ONE HOME UNDER GOD

JACK R. TAYLOR

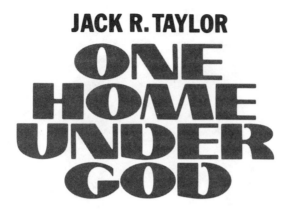

ONE HOME UNDER GOD

BROADMAN PRESS
NASHVILLE, TENNESSEE

4252-22
ISBN: 0-8054-5222-2

Library of Congress Catalog Card Number: 73-91609
Dewey Decimal Classification: 301.42
Printed in the United States of America

DEDICATION

TO THE FAMILY . . .
> Mine, Yours, Everyone's EVERYWHERE
> God's last line of defense for our nation!

This volume is written with the belief and toward the commitment that our one great hope is found in the homes of America.

May the pages of this volume introduce you and your family to the miracle of Spirit-controlled family living, the nearest and clearest picture of heaven in this universe.

CONTENTS

Introduction

In our well-worded Pledge of Allegiance we say, ". . . one nation under God, Indivisible, with liberty and justice for all." In the not-too-distant past we added "under God." Somebody realized that if we were to be one nation, indivisible, it was mockery to think that it could be maintained in any other position than "under God." Now, we are realizing more than ever that if we are to be "one nation under God," we must have *homes under God.* The home is that basic building block of which our nation is made. As the home goes, so goes the nation.

If we are to have one nation under God, we must begin with ONE HOME UNDER GOD. May the following pages serve to secure the place where you live as ONE HOME UNDER GOD.

This volume is not intended to be a thorough treatise on home and family life. It is rather an adventure into the struggles and heartaches of one American home and on to victory in Jesus Christ. My family and I have come to discover that for the most part our problems are fairly near the same the world over. We have come through some deep (and sometimes dark) waters and I know that there are more ahead, but through these times we have learned some vital lessons that we feel must be shared.

This is not a neatly arrayed plan to solve all family ills and bring your home to a heaven-like state in a few easy steps. We can promise, however, that there are some secrets which, when believed and applied, will make an immediate difference in your family life.

Many wonderful things are happening in America today. There seems to be blowing the positive and fresh winds of revival. The ministry of the Holy Spirit is being discussed and explored more today than perhaps any generation since the beginning of Christendom. But with all that we see, the crumbling of the home as a basic institution of our society continues to be an item of priority concern. A revival that does not move into the homes of America is destined for brevity of life or, at the best, only limited success. On the other hand, a revival that touches the home will touch the whole of our nation's life.

The home is America's heart. The home is under attack and shows signs of weakening. The home is in trouble. America has heart trouble!

This is not time for farcical formulas or pious platitudes. We need something deeper than mere morality. What is done needs to be done immediately. The unsteady heartbeat of this mighty nation needs to be checked by the infallible Word of God to determine procedures for recovery. Simple prescriptions must be given and resolute steps must be taken to follow the divine order for the home outlined in the Bible.

We can never expect this to happen on a corporate level. It will never be legislated or forced upon us. You and I in our individual homes must return to God's family life-styles. If it takes the whole collapse of the system on which our nation stands to bring us to the point of willingness, I am convinced that God loves us enough to allow it to happen. In this sense now is the time to start—with you, right where you are. This volume cannot be read objectively. You are subjectively involved now! The future of your nation rests with your home. It may well be now or never!

So you see, it is more than just a matter of bringing your home to its maximum state of happiness. It is the creation of an atmosphere through which the God of heaven can move into your house and through your house to the neighborhood and the world. I fully believe that this is his plan!

The perils of our time, many of them totally unique to the fading years of the twentieth century, will find their corresponding purposes in your house as it becomes "One home under God." Allow these confessions, reports, and suggestions to be used as the tools in an intense investigation of your home, its pressures and pleasures, its purposes and its problems, until God shows you all that a home can be.

May God grant you and your family through the reading of these pages a revival in your home. As that happens, it will not be long before you have revival on the job, revival at school, revival in the neighborhood, and revival in the church. Now is the time!

If not now . . . when?

If not here . . . where?

If not you and I . . . who?

JACK R. TAYLOR

Of all human relationships, none are more vital and enduring than those of home and family. Love and marriage, the joys of parenthood and family ties are the bases of all that is best in life . . . the supreme happiness.

SELECTED

He is happiest who finds peace in his home.

GOETHE

The greatest of all arts is the art of living together.

WILLIAM LYON PHELPS

1 Marriage . . . the End and the Beginning

God's plan had a wonderful beginning,
Man ruined his chances by sinning,
They say that the story will end in God's glory
But at present it seems the other side's winning!

The Human Horror

Man is staring in shock at the near-collapse of all his systems. They have not worked to create for him his hoped-for utopia. He is an enigma to himself. He can achieve in one area so marvelously as to predict with hairbreadth precision the location of the heavenly bodies for centuries to come, but cannot control his own generation.

He can lift a towering manned rocket into space and with perfect accuracy land a man on the moon to pluck him off again and bring him back home . . . to a home that is literally falling apart. There is not a single problem in the millions of miles of space travel and touring about on the surface of the moon, but back from outer space the problems of inner space in his home seem unsolvable!

With postgraduate advancements in every field of technology man has yet to move out of kindergarten in the management of his own affairs at home. Science has perfected the art of communication until we could carry on conversations with interstellar neighbors if we had them, but we have lost the art of communication in the home!

13

We are witnesses to the obvious failure of man's systems.

The *educational* system, though sophisticated in our own measurements, is not producing the desired ends, because in the midst of the educational process we are losing our sense of decency, morality, and human respect.

The *economic* system seems to be on the verge of tottering from top-heaviness. If the doctor pronounces you as "sound as a dollar," you had better make immediate funeral arrangements. We have not seen the worst yet.

The *political* system has not only lost the respect of the populace for the most part, but has lost respect for itself. If you cannot trust yourself, who can you trust? Disillusionment abounds. Panic fills the atmosphere.

In the midst of the pandemonium the *religious* system scrambles for some comforting identity, but languishes sickeningly in the mire of its tradition-bound slough of despond. Its goal, once to *thrive*, has depreciated now at best to a hope to *survive*.

Has anyone in this nightmare anything to say? Is there not a turnaround somewhere on this maddening route to ruin? Is there no formula to be given that will work? These seem to be man's cries as he views the debris of his own doing, the seeming finality of his own failure.

From out of the pages of the Bible comes the answer. God did not make us like this! He does not find delight in this human disaster. It was not so in the beginning. We stand at the unpleasant *end* of history. It is well that we review the *beginning*.

The Divine Design

Why did God do it? The answer is not as simple as some theologians have wanted to make it. The reasons for creation are locked away in the heart of God to be revealed at his desire in his time for his "forever" family. In the meanwhile we have to settle for some solid speculations. Among these suggestions the following seem fitting:

God desired to extend divine life. "Let us make man in our image" was the declaration of Elohim. (The divine trinity is suggested by the use of the name *Elohim*, Gen. 1:26a.) God prepared creation for its crowning deposit—man. That man would bear family likeness to the godhead. He would be a picture of the trinity. He would be an extension of the life of God.

God desired to express his nature. It was in God's image and after his likeness that man was created. His very actions and nature would be a revelation of the nature of his Creator. Paul declared in Romans 1:19, "Because that which may be known of God was manifest in them; for God hath shewed it unto them." It was through man and his offspring that the character of Holy God was to be revealed. That is the purpose of redeemed man today.

God desired to exhibit his dominion. And God said, "Let them have dominion over the fish of the sea, and over the fowl of the air, and over the cattle, and over all the earth, and over every creeping thing that creepeth upon the earth" (Gen. 1:26*b*). Man was created to reign, but only under the dominion of God. As long as man would remain under him who was over him, all that was under God (which was everything) would also be under man. Thus, into a world where Satan sought to usurp authority, God introduced man and the family to be used as a means of extending divine life, expressing divine nature, and exhibiting divine dominion.

Focus on the Family

In the first creation narrative in Genesis 1 we are told, "God created man in his own image, in the image of God created he him." We are then told, ". . . male and female created he them." Some of the most vital truth for the family is found on the ground around this verse (1:27). God did not ever have the intention that man be alone. There is a sense in which he was created complete with the woman who would later be *taken from* man in order to be *given to* man. God created man in his own image. The whole man is comprised of the male and the female. Not one alone, but both together were made to reign and continue in dominion over God's creation.

The Creation of the Family

Good, good, good, good, good, good, NOT good, VERY GOOD! Six times in the first chapter of Genesis at various stages of creation the

word "good" is used to describe the picture to the eyes of God. "And
God saw that it was good" (vv. 4,10,12,18,21,25). Then in verse 18
of chapter 2 when man was still alone we are confronted with the first
"not good" of the Bible. "And the Lord God said, It is not good that
man should be alone." Then in the description of the earlier account
of the creation with Adam and Eve cooperating together in Genesis
1:31 we observe, "And God saw everything that he has made and,
behold, it was very good."

Thus is born the first and only institution which predates the fall
of man, the home. It was designed to carry out the purposes of God
in *extending* his life, *expressing* his character, and *exhibiting* his dominion. It was to be God's most effective tool against the devil right
in his own territory. It is to be a kingdom of *right* within a kingdom
of *wrong,* a kingdom of *light* within a kingdom of *darkness.*

We have taken notice as we have read the creation story that God
introduced the fact of evil to Adam before Eve came on the scene.
God told Adam of the trees of the garden. Among them was the tree
of life in the midst of the garden and the tree of knowledge of good
and evil. Adam was to have freedom to eat of every tree including
the tree of life except the tree of knowledge of good and evil. Man
was to live by divine revelation, not human knowledge.

It was immediately after this warning that God brought all the
animals to Adam to be named. God had doubtlessly informed Adam
that he was going to make a helpmeet for him. (She was to be not
just a mate, but a *helpmate* fitted for Adam, intellectually, morally,
spiritually, and physically.) Surely Adam went to work with eager
anticipation naming the animals, watching with intense interest for
his "helpmeet." But alas, she did not come by this means. "But for
Adam there was not found an help meet for him" (Gen. 2:20).

In order to get man completed and prepared for the coming of his
helpmeet, God administered the first anesthesia and performed the
first major surgery. God took from Adam's side a rib and from it
fashioned by his own skill, the woman. He then brought her to Adam.
Adam then held a special thanksgiving service in which he declared
his formal reception of the woman. "This is now bone of my bones,
and flesh of my flesh: she shall be called woman, because she was

taken out of man" (v. 23). This was his doxology of acceptance!

The Commands for the Family

The blessing of God upon his creation obviously included the capacity to reproduce after its kind. The first instance of blessing is recorded in Genesis 1:22 and is followed immediately by the command, "Be fruitful and multiply." In Genesis 1:24 after the second instance of blessing is recorded there is a fivefold command:
Be fruitful,
> multiply,
>> replenish the earth,
>>> subdue it,
and continue to have dominion over it. This was God's master strategy for the continuous victory of good over evil and the home was to be the secret weapon!

Adam had some concept of the purpose of woman and of future generations when he said, "Therefore shall a man leave his father and mother, and shall cleave unto his wife: and they shall be one flesh" (v. 24). The primacy of the home in society and the nature of the family relationship is presented here. Man and wife were to exist as one flesh. They were to live, decide, worship, and serve as one flesh. Woman was taken *from* man, given *to* man, in order to *complete* man. A classic statement is ascribed to C. H. Spurgeon: "Woman was not taken out of man's head to be lorded over by him, or from his feet to be trampled on by him, but from his side to be equal with him, from under his arm to be protected by him, and from near his heart to be loved by him."

But as glorious as was man's beginning, there was trouble on the horizon.

Chaos in the Family

Wherever there is trouble, there is breakdown in authority. It was true with the first sin and will be true with the last one. Eve made several mistakes in Genesis 3. Adam had obviously shared the warning of God about the forbidden tree with Eve. She either forgot or had never been deeply impressed enough with the warning to be moved by it. The wife of today may well refrain from serious error by studying the mistakes of Eve.

First, she was isolated from her husband. He was her protection. She was his completion. The devil knew that if he could get to her, he could eventually get to man. This has been his method down through the centuries. If he can cause a gap between husband and wife, he can begin his sordid work whether that gap be geographical, moral, intellectual, physical, or spiritual. The devil had the advantage of having her alone for his work of deceit.

Second, she communicated with the devil when she should have deferred to her husband. After all he was the one who had heard the original command regarding the forbidden tree. It was he who was the likely one to confront the half-truths of the devil head-on with the direct quotes of God in his mind. But Eve usurped a position which was not hers. She should have consulted her teacher-husband immediately.

Third, she turned from revelation to reason. This is precisely what is happening today in our world. Mankind is living off the tree of knowledge. Reason demands explanation. Revelation demands nothing but obedience. When the devil had persuaded Eve to look again at the tree instead of revelation, he was on the way to conquering her. "When she saw . . ." was the prelude to her downfall. When she decided to think for herself, her soulish powers went into action. She quickly saw that it was good for food, pleasant to the eye, and desired to make one wise. She had jumped the track of divine revelation and was running headlong down the path of human reason.

Fourth, she made a decision entirely independent from her husband. Their dominion was to be together. Thus their decisions should have been together. They were part and parcel of each other. Each was the completion of the other. The devil could not deal with both of them together. They were more than his equal in the will of God. But the power unit of the first family was weakened by independence and individuality. Eve sinned and Adam followed. Paul observes in his teaching about the woman's responsibility in 1 Timothy that Adam was not deceived (2:14). Chaos resulted. From that failure has come every failure of mankind.

Condemnation upon the World

With chaos in the family there were multiple judgments on the world. Man and woman were banished from the utopia of God's creation. They were thrown into a world in rebellion. Man was to eke out a living by the sweat of his face. The woman was to be saved by childbearing. She was to capitulate to her husband's desires. He was to rule over her.

But with all that happened in the fall of man, there is no hint that God would abandon the family! It was to continue to be his tool against the devil. While the earth would bring forth thorns and thistles and man would carry on his battle against the elements and a rebellious world, the family would still be the basic unit in God's society.

Consummate Hope of Civilization

There was nothing wrong with God's plan. It was right from the start. It was *man* and not the *plan* that failed. Therefore, there is no reason to abandon the plan. The plan was to implement the purposes of God through the family. The only hope of restoring any semblance of purpose to our generation is to be found in the family. No institutions in our society shall rise above the home. As the home goes, so goes the morality, the business, and the government. As the home goes, so goes the nation. God, give us Christian homes!

Closing Challenge

As you come to the end of this opening chapter, I remind you that we are talking about *your* home. Only as the weight of the issue rests upon your awareness, your convictions, your willingness to bring your home under God's scrutiny, will there be any decisive action on your part. The theological background is now behind us. The practical is just ahead of us. We have seen the beginning and we stand near the end. While prophecy is going to be fulfilled, and there is nothing we can do to change that, we may be certain that the nearest spot to heaven in these hellish days will continue to be "one home under God!" May the following pages serve to help God help you make your home just such a place.

A man's house is his fortress in a warring world where a woman's hand buckles on his armor in the morning and soothes his fatigue and wounds at night.

FRANK CRANE

2 The Miracle at Our House

When home is ruled by the Word of God,
Angels might be asked to stay with us,
And they would not find themselves
Out of their element.—*C. H. Spurgeon*

I am often asked if I believe in miracles. It is a common declaration in some theological circles that the age of miracles has passed. For those who believe this, the age of miracles *has* passed. For them there will be no miracles. According to their faith, so be it unto them. I will be glad to leave the technical discussion of the pros and cons of modern miracles to someone else. In the meanwhile I am too busy enjoying miracles to argue about them! You see, I live in a miracle. What God has done in my home is a miracle of such proportions that I would have to see nothing else in order to be a believer in miracles.

In fact I live *with* a miracle. I am married to a miracle. Two miracles call me father every day. My wife and children are veritable living miracles. If in this chapter I could lift out of my heart what is there and put it on these pages for you to see and feel, I would need to do nothing more. For God has wrought in my home such a work of grace that I feel a mandate to share it with you. Wherever we have shared this, we have seen dozens of couples across the nation come into a newfound joy in their married lives.

21

The devil will go to any means to destroy your homelife and your home. If he cannot completely destroy it, he will bring it to a permanent state of confusion and chaos. If he can do nothing else, he will settle for anything short of a submission of the couple to each other which brings the power of God upon their marriage.

For almost seventeen years the secret I am about to share with you was kept from me. I have shared this in part in a chapter of my first book, *The Key to Triumphant Living,* under the title, "Revival in the Home." I first shared this experience less than six months after it happened. I can testify that as the years pass, the experience and the discovery become sweeter because the results of that discovery continue to shape the life of my family. Praise the Lord!

We had been married more than seventeen years. There was never any doubt but that the Lord had led us together. No human would have even thought of it or have been able to put it together! She was from the city; I was from the country. She was expressive and an extrovert. I was rather quiet and (believe it or not) an introvert! Our reactions most of the time formed a perfect balance . . . we always reacted exactly opposite to each other. Had you asked either of us at the time, we would have probably assured you that ours was a genuinely happy home. But had you come to spend a day or a week with us, you would have wondered.

In 1970 the Spirit of God touched down in our area and in our church in a glorious time of revival. God had begun a revival in my life several years before as I had been awakened to the only hope of the Christian. . . . "Christ in Me!" The Holy Spirit had continued to make Jesus real in, to, and through me for all those years. When Barbara (my wife) saw that something had happened in me, she began to take notice and investigate. "I will just wait and see," she seemed to be saying. Then God began to do a work in her. With the revival, the Holy Spirit continued to do a glorious work inside both of us.

But to the surprise of both of us the little things that we thought were around no longer, the resentments, the hang-ups, the fears, began to boil to the surface. Our victory was so wonderful, everywhere except at home! We seemed unable to apply what we knew from new revelations the Spirit had given us to our household. We would pray, especially in a family crisis, and things would be better for a few weeks, but then a new crisis would come that would make it clear that total victory was not there. God brought us to a fearful experience which caused such a transformation that we often find ourselves talking about it as if it were just yesterday.

In the midst of wonderful revival the devil was doing his work. While God was moving and souls were being saved and we were being used, there was yet a wedge between us as husband and wife. It reached an all-time low as far as crisis was concerned in December of 1970. A simple little misunderstanding arose over a matter that was not a serious issue at all. However, it did stem from a problem of my failing to give attention to my wife as a husband should in the presence of others. I knew right away that something was wrong. Do you ever have those times when you know that something is wrong and there is no obvious reason for knowing? The atmosphere clearly told me that all was not well and I knew that on the way home I could expect a lively discussion. I was not disappointed. In a few minutes we were on our way home and the discussion moved quickly from the symptom to the real problem. Discussion of the real problem was more uncomfortable than discussing the symptom. The symptom was I had not paid attention to her in the presence of others. The problem was that I was in a position where I could never know or be able to pay her proper attention until something happened in my life with reference to my wife.

Resentments arose, tempers flared, appropriate events from the past were recalled as they would serve to advantage us against each other. After a while we were awakened to the fearful fact that we were no longer able to communicate. We had reached a dead end! It was like a nightmare to me. I could see the end of the whole thing. If something did not happen, there would be tragedy.

This had all taken place on our way home from the other side of our city. On the way home I drove by the church and unlocked the doors and we walked into the darkened auditorium. We had labored here for over thirteen years and the blessings of God had been poured out mightily. I knew as we walked in that place that night that unless God performed a miracle, we could not continue. We walked together down the dark aisle and found ourselves kneeling at the altar at the front of the church. We had little to say in prayer and we wondered after the way we talked with each other a little while before, if there was a bit of mockery in trying to talk with God at all. I don't remember what we prayed, but somewhere in it was a prayer for a miracle in our home.

We went home and Barbara took the baby-sitter home. When she returned, she began to read the Bible beginning at Ephesians 5. I was lying on the bed reading something else. All of a sudden she literally tossed the Bible over to me and said, "Is this what is wrong? Am I just not submissive to you?" Not desiring to make a bad matter worse, I softly replied that I did not think she had been. She was referring to Ephesians 5:22 which says, "Wives, submit yourselves unto your own husbands, as unto the Lord." We had dealt with that verse before and thought the matter was settled. What we didn't know was that the whole matter could not be settled on that single response. I might add that when we had discussed it before, I was a little less than cordial as I demanded her to be submissive to me or else. The relationship that followed that "Commitment" was something less than ideal.

But that night things were different. Somehow we both must have felt that there would be a turning point in our marriage that very evening. All of a sudden things began to happen. We began to communicate with each other through the pages of the Bible. The Holy Spirit filled that room and at that moment he was everything but a Sweet, Sweet Spirit. There was a sternness about his presence that seemed to say more than we had ever heard before. My eyes dropped down on the context as well as the text. In Ephesians 5:17 the last seven words are "What the will of the Lord is." Then there is the command in verse 18 to "be filled with the Spirit." Then there is a picture of harmonious communication in verse 19 and continuous thanksgiving in verse 20.

Have you ever felt that the Holy Spirit had just inserted a verse in the Bible since you had last read it? That is how I felt that night as I looked down to see the next verse which said, "submitting yourselves one to another in the fear of God." With the reading of those last three words, "fear of God," there seemed to have swept into that room a cold wind of warning to both of us. The thought hit me like a ten-ton truck. *I had been expecting her to submit herself to me without any submission on my part.* There must have been some protest in my spirit. Was I not in authority? How could authority be submissive? Would it not be at the expense of losing the position of authority? But suddenly it began to dawn. Had not God in Christ submitted himself to a cross for me? Did not Jesus pay the supreme price to be my authority? The very act of giving up his life for me gave him the right to be my authority.

There seems to have been some protest in Barbara's spirit also as she said, "Well, I think I could submit to you, but you have a lousy record." Those were, as I recall, her exact words. I replied, "Well, your record is not so hot itself." We were both right, but that was not the issue. Spiritual communication was still going on as the Lord reminded us in that Scripture that past records had nothing to do with mutual submission. *We were to submit ourselves to each other in the fear of the Lord.* There need be no other reason. There is no reason to wait on needed improvement or a period of reconstruction. We were faced with the necessity of submitting to each other "in the fear of the Lord" and not on the basis of a pair of "lousy" records.

I knew at that moment that with all that I had tried to do to make Barbara feel that I loved her and needed her, I had not done the one thing that must be done to prove this. I had never been a part of the "miracle of mutual submission." With the realization that this verse applies to body truth in the church, I will leave that discussion for another book. The import here is within the context of marriage. We had fallen into the peril of discussing "my ministry" and the fact that it must be protected at all costs. She often prayed that if she were ever a hindrance to "my ministry" that God would take her. What we did not realize was that it was not "my" ministry but "his," and it involved both of us. In reality she and the children were my ministry. Having come to this realization, I was willing for the first time to really submit myself to her as her husband. I was willing to let God make me the husband she needed and the father my children needed if it meant leaving the ministry. I was willing to take a job plowing fields or digging ditches, if that was what it would take. My family had become more important than all the things to which I had found myself intensely committed.

I said to my wife, "Honey, I am willing to submit myself to you." She was as willing as was I. We slipped down on our knees at the side of our bed and formally gave ourselves to each other in the fear of the Lord. We both knew that something vital had happened. As I look back on it now I am glad that the Lord did not drop the whole load of emotions on us then. The change was miraculous, immediate, and permanent. We communicated as never before. She submitted as never before in all things. I could hardly believe it. After our mutual submission she eagerly announced that she was choosing of her own will to be in submission to me as unto the Lord.

If the joy that comes immediately upon the miracle of mutual submission is glorious, the implementation of the miracle into every part of married life is joy unspeakable. Like salvation, mutual submission is both an *event* and a *process*. There are dozens of opportunities to invoke it and apply it. The joy increases as circumstances, reactions, and situations come under the light of this miracle. As the light comes there comes the delight of knowing that once a couple is in mutual submission to each other and in obedience to God, all things work to their good.

Allow me in the closing paragraphs to summarize this miracle of mutual submission. We were both, as far as we knew, in submission to God. We loved the Lord and loved each other and were trying very hard to be what each other needed. Yet there was a struggle within our marriage that neither of us could identify. That evening we came face to face with the fact that we had never really submitted ourselves to each other. As a result we were not to each other all that we were made to be. I believe that on that evening God gave us both a revelation and it came to both of us simultaneously. Christ was in her and Christ was in me. We wanted him to be Lord in both of us. When we released him within us to fully love the other, it was an interrelationship of love. . . . Christ in her loving Christ in me. The submissive Savior in each of us was submitting himself to himself. We began to see Christ in each other, feel Christ in each other, and respond to Christ in each other!

We had known that when two people marry, they were supposed to be "one." We had trouble for all those years deciding which one! On that night we found that it was neither one . . . but Christ himself. Only the white-hot heat of a Savior's love can take two uniquely different objects (husband and wife) and melt them together to the point that it is impossible to tell where one leaves off and the other begins. Christ is one . . . never two. When there is conflict between two people, they are no longer acting as one. Someone besides Christ has invaded the domain that belongs exclusively to him. Prevailing honesty will discover which one has resurrected and unity can reign again.

Obviously the experience of most couples will not come as it did to us. We were both together and God brought us into a realization together. More often it will be the wife or the husband who will come to the realization of the necessity of a mutual submission. If you are the one who first recognizes the need for submission and that recognition becomes spirit-given conviction, remember, . . . the righteous make concession (as in Abraham's case with Lot) and it is *your* move! Those under this category will find help in the chapter entitled "Wives, Submit . . . Husbands, Love!"

Questions for You as You Close This Chapter

Are there indications in your marriage that you have experienced this miracle of mutual submission?

Are there indications that you have not experienced it?

Is this concept new to you?

Are there any protests in your spirit to this concept?

Look them over closely and examine them and ask if they are valid in the light of the Scripture.

Husband, are your job and your future more important to you than your family? Do your schedule and interests bear out the truth of your answer?

Are there now pockets of resistance between you as husband and wife? Are there areas that keep recurring as problem points?

Husband, do you consider it a dangerous concession to make to tell your wife that you are submitting yourself to her as Christ did the church? Would you dare to do it now?

Wife, do you feel that you are giving up rights as you yield in the moment of mutual submission?

You may need to lay this volume aside for now and live up to the light which you have been given. The remainder of this book will be a greater blessing if you have discovered the "miracle of mutual submission" early in the reading.

This chapter is followed by three refrains. The first is from my wife, Barbara. The second is from my daughter, Tamara, the third is from my son, Timothy. I believe that when you have read them, you will know why I wanted them to write a part of this book.

Barbara's Refrain

There have been several times in my Christian life when I have asked God for a miracle. With greater urgency than ever before I asked God for a miracle in my home. I discovered that before God can work a miracle *for* us, he usually has to work one *in* us. I prayed for a specific miracle in my relationship with my husband. Instead of an immediate miracle, God began to bring me into submission that I had found so repulsive to my mind for all the years of our marriage.

That night in 1970 is a night we will never forget. We had reached an impasse in our communications. I knew that we had to have a miracle. I could not imagine what the alternative to that miracle might have been.

God had been working in my life, bringing me to the end of self by which I had been ruled all the years of our marriage. I had been experiencing deliverance from many things in my life that I seemed to have had because of family characteristics and upbringing. I grew up to be self-willed and independent. I was running my own life at a very early age and experienced much jealousy, selfishness, and bitterness. It was no choice with me; I was all of this by nature and without effort.

God caused me to see in print what I had to do before I would believe him. When my eyes fell on the Scripture in Ephesians 5:22, the Holy Spirit immediately took control. Conditions were right for him to work. I had been praying that the Lord would make me the wife, the mother, and the Christian that he wanted me to be. I had confessed my sins up-to-date and wanted God to do a work in my life. I knew that I could not and would not go on as I had.

I saw so many things that my husband should be doing and wasn't. I thought that most of the fault was in him. What I did not see was that in failing to take my rightful place in submission to God and to him under God, I was keeping him from becoming what he should be.

That night I asked Jack if my not obeying Ephesians 5:22 was my problem. "Am I just not being submissive," I asked. He replied that he did not think I was. We began right there to communicate and the presence of the Holy Spirit fearfully filled the room. I knew that I must obey . . . that we both must obey. I submitted to the Christ who lives in my husband and he to the Christ that lives in me. We came to God's order and plan for our marriage. Jack received me and I received Jack. We discovered the secret of becoming one in marriage. Two people who were distinctly individual in their personalities became one in the Lord.

It has been such an exciting experience and sometimes fearful. God continues to teach me about areas of submission to Jack, my husband, my lord and priest, through allowing me to learn true submission to God, my Father through Jesus in Jack and me.

God has been pleased to bless us in every way imaginable during the last three years especially. Our relationship as husband and wife has yielded more joy than all the other seventeen years combined.

Praise the Lord.

Tammy's Refrain

I was twelve years old when it happened. I want to tell you what I saw and what happened in my life because of it. I knew that we were just a normal family and there was nothing in our home that I did not see in any other home.

Mom and Dad were always real busy and we seemed to have little time together as a family. When we did get together, it seemed that we had a hard time getting along with each other and making decisions. We did not pray together often. Mom and Dad often had open disagreements in front of brother and me. Sometimes Dad would come in with the problems of the church and take out his frustrations on us.

But something happened between Mom and Dad. The first two things that I saw were Mom becoming submissive and Dad beginning to treat her like he should.

We began to pray through our problems and spend more time together as a family. We began to do things together and enjoy it more. There was more discipline and I did not resent it like I did before. Dad and Mom seemed to discipline us to help us, instead of taking their anger out on us.

When Dad and Mom got into line, Tim and I had to get under authority also. We discussed the matter of authority as a family and I saw it as a matter that related us to God. I felt more love from my parents and because of this, I felt more love for my parents.

Before this happened in our home I did not know what the Spirit-filled life was. After Mom and Dad got right with each other, they began to explain what the Holy Spirit could do in the lives of children like us.

We began to communicate and understand each other as we never had before. It was fun being together as a family. About this time our vacation time came and we were driving and talking as we drove. The more we talked, the more we understood and the more we wanted God to do what he wanted to do in us. We all decided that we would drive alongside the road and have a prayer meeting. For the first time in my Christian life I asked God to fill me with his Holy Spirit and take complete control of my life.

As God began to fill me with his Spirit and take control of me I have begun to witness his guidance in every area of my life. As the Spirit led me, I felt impressed to go to a private Christian school where the Bible is taught and I have the privilege of studying Greek in order to understand the Bible better. All the teachers are very understanding and we pray before every class that God might have his way in every class period.

I prayed about running for cheerleader and the Lord allowed me to win. I also prayed about singing in a special group in our church called "The Living Dead" (named from Galatians 2:20) and the Lord allowed me to be selected.

I praise the Lord for what happened in my home, in my parents, and for what is happening in my life. I have never resented being a preacher's daughter, but now I enjoy it more than I ever have.

I want my life to count for the Lord. I want him to take my life and do with it what he wants to do. I believe that he has called me to be a missionary and wherever he leads me, I will go.

NOTE: Tammy, at this writing is fifteen years old. She was saved when she was seven while going through the course provided by our church in the Bible Memory Association. She is a sophomore in the San Antonio Christian School.

Timmy's Refrain

I was saved when I was six years old and almost ten when God began to do something in our home that was new. We had a pretty good relationship as a family, but nothing like we have now.

I noticed that Mom and Dad seemed to have a different relationship. Tammy and I began to get along better. We were happier with each other, . . . all of us.

My Dad has always spanked me when I needed it, but sometimes he got real mad when he did it. This has changed. It still hurts when he spanks me, but it is done in love and I know that it is God's will.

When Dad told us that we would be helping to write a part of this book, I thought about writing about "The Lord and a Large White Belt." The reason I thought of this title was that it takes both the Lord and my Dad to keep me straight. The Lord does it in a number of ways and my Dad uses (sometimes) a large white belt. I am thankful for both.

Tammy and I used to fight a lot before, but now we seldom ever fight. Our relationship is not perfect, but it is improving every day.

When I was younger, I had a terrible temper. I asked the Lord to fill me with his Holy Spirit and he is keeping it under control most of the time.

It all started with my parents and what happens to them has a great influence on their children. I have chosen to follow the Lord in everything. I am happy when God can tell me things and help me in decisions.

In the fall of 1972 Tammy felt led of the Lord to enroll in a private Christian school. I did not want to give up football and other sports, so I went back to public school. I did not make it through three days before the Lord got hold of me. He would not let me enjoy school and I could not wait to get out of school and get home. I was miserable. One day I told the Lord that if he wanted me to go to the Christian school, he would make me feel sick. I was sick when I came home from school. Mom and I had prayed together and when Dad got in we had prayer together. He asked God to heal me right then if it was his will that I go to the Christian school. I decided to follow the Lord and he healed me right then. This year has been my best year ever in school.

I love the Lord and enjoy serving him. I want to do what he wants me to do. I do not know just what he wants me to be. I have some interest in being a lawyer and some interest in being a preacher.

Even though my Dad has been gone much of the time, I have been with him more than I ever have. We have made some trips together and have gotten better acquainted as a family.

What happened in our home made a great difference in all of us for which I am grateful.

NOTE: Timmy is presently thirteen years of age and is in the eighth grade at San Antonio Christian School.

Nature makes her a woman; election, a wife; but only grace can make her subject. One of the greatest things a woman can do for her husband and her country is to give her husband his rightful place as the head of their home.

BYFIELD

The most important thing that a father can do for his children is to love their mother.

THEODORE HESBURGH

3 Wives, Submit . . . Husbands, Love!

No wife ever had a satisfactorily wedded life who did not look up to and reverence her husband.—*Alexander McClaren*

And you husbands, show the same kind of love to your wives as Christ showed to the church when he died for her (Eph. 5:25, TLB).

God's directions are always simple! To the wife he gives one word and to the husband one. If you would be a successful, happy, fulfilled, and godly wife or husband, you must reckon with these words.

We have discussed the "miracle of mutual submission." This, however, is only the platform upon which the superstructure of a successful marriage is built. No organization can function properly without submission. Submission suggests authority. The whole of nature operates on authority and submission. To take these factors away would be to destroy the whole realm of nature.

The Word for Wives . . . Submit!

When God assigned woman to a place of submission, it was not for punishment, but for fulfillment. God is never interested in *prolonging punishment,* but in *fulfilling purpose.* He said to woman, "And

34

thy desire shall be to thy husband, and he shall rule over thee" (Gen. 3:16).

There is no doubt in the Bible about the role of the woman in the home.

"Wives, submit yourselves unto your own husbands as unto the Lord" (Eph. 5:22).

"Therefore as the church is subject unto Christ, so let the wives be to their own husbands in every thing" (Eph. 5:24).

"Wives, submit yourselves unto your own husbands, as it is fit in the Lord" (Col. 3:18).

"Likewise ye wives, be in subjection to your own husbands. For after this manner in the old time, the holy women also, who trusted God, adorned themselves, being in subjection into their own husbands" (1 Pet. 3:1,5).

Look at it this way, wife. You want to be treated like a queen . . . right? Only wives of kings can be guaranteed that they will be treated like queens. (However that is!) There are several alternatives open. You could try to get yourself a king, but then that would not be right. The shortest route to becoming a queen is that of crowning your very own husband as king! You say, "Crown *that* as a king?" You remember that Sarah called Abraham "lord." She crowned him the king of her household.

You will discover, dear wife, that the moment you crown your husband king, he begins to feel the part. He begins to look for a queen. You are the prime suspect. He takes a new look at you after you have crowned him the king. He designates you his queen and begins to treat you like what you are.

The Disaster of a Dominating Wife

Let's talk negatively for a bit! Many women are aggressive by nature and if the Word is not obeyed at this point this aggressiveness will give her the lead in family life. It is done without deliberation or effort. After a time of domination, whether intentional or unintentional, her aggression will likely become more intense and the husband more retiring. As she grows older she will come to a time when she wishes she had a leaning post. But she discovers that she has created a situation where she, herself, is the leaning post. This is the point where many a wife has found her love turning to resentment for the man she forced to become a party to her refusal to be a submissive wife. The woman was not made to dominate and when she does, there will be a time when she will loathe the situation which finds her in control. Thus, there is the disaster of a wife's unmet needs.

True authority is constructed on truth. As strange as it sounds, an unsubmissive and authoritative wife does not have true authority. One *has* authority only when he or she is *under* authority. Our adversary, the devil, is delighted with a situation such as this for he has working room where truth does not prevail. Thus, we see that the unsubmissive wife not only presents the problem of being unable to be the true authority for the children, but that of preventing the husband and father from being the true authority. The children are angered at the situation without knowing why. There is confusion at best and total chaos at worst. There is the disaster of deficient discipline.

On the negative side I have one other thing to add. To my memory I have never counselled with a homosexual who did not have the above situation in his homelife. A dominating mother is generally a factor to be considered in cases of homosexuality. The reason is not certain, but in all probability there is identification with the stronger of the couple and some resentment for the weaker, thus there comes a confusion of sexual roles as a boy and later as a man.

Submission, Authority, and Coequality

The fear of many a woman at the approach of submission is that thought of becoming a slave. This is not what God has in mind. In everything with any semblance of order there are both headship and authority. It is so in our bodies. There is a head and there is a body. I never look upon them as in competition or conflict. They are complementary.

Submission is not an admission of inferiority; it is the acknowledgement of God's order. Submission to authority does not cancel coequality. One's position in the chain of authority does not have bearing on the matter of equality. For instance, I am under the authority of the President of the United States, but we are coequal in its system.

My submission to the fact of his authority is not a confession of my inferiority to him. Paul said, "There is neither Jew nor Greek, there is neither bond nor free, there is neither male nor female: for ye are all one in Christ Jesus" (Gal. 3:28).

The confusion of "submission" with "inferiority" is the basic mistake with movements today aimed at "emancipating womanhood." People do not have to be alike to be equal. The best way to destroy anything is to take away its basic reason for being and making it like something else. To seek to make woman just like man is to destroy her reason for being. God did not take Adam's rib and make another man. He made a helper fitted to his needs. It is neither emancipating nor advantageous to seek to take a woman out of her position as a woman and make her like man. Let's face it. Man and woman are different in more ways than one and many of those ways are unseen to all but God. We cannot foretell what disaster will come as a result of the demonic attempt to make man and woman *alike* under the guise of making them *equal.*

Lars J. Granberg in his book, *For Adults Only,* gives the following report: "At a recent convention of the Academy of Psychosomatic Medicine a respected Eastern Seaboard physician and mental health specialist claimed that the rising incidence of sexual frigidity in wives, sexual impotency in husbands, and homosexuality in children is largely due to 'role change', i.e., women taking the part of men in society and at home. He further stated that wherever women could be helped to find a truly feminine role, the situation was resolved."

Why Me First? (A Wife)

I have asked that question myself. Why does the command in Ephesians 5:22 for the wife to be in submission to the husband appear before the command in Ephesians 5:25 for the husband to love the wife? That is a very good question. I do not know that anyone has the answer for certain. I have found some real joy in the following speculation:

> Wife, you have been gifted by God with an awesome dynamic. You were taken from man. Without you he is incomplete. You have been given to him to make him complete. Just

because God has put you first, however, is not the guarantee of fulfillment. It takes your choice and your commitment. You are to your husband either a *crippler* or a *completer*. You have the power to do either . . . the capacity to keep him crippled (or incomplete) or continuously complete. You have been commanded to submit to your husband because it is in God's order and in that order God has gifted you with the awesome power of a submissive spirit. If you and your husband have experienced the miracle of mutual submission, now under the influence of your submission, he is released to be a total *man* and to make you a *total* woman. No man or woman is total who is not fitting into God's order. If mutual submission has not been established in your home, you may be sure that through your submission to your husband, God is then free to "get at" him without interference from you. You will be surprised at how God can work under such circumstances. You will have moved from a "complicity in the crime" to a blessed "cooperation with God."

So wife, it's your turn! The whole thing is in your hands. It may not seem fair to your logical mind, but there it is!

Becoming Submissive

Any woman, regardless of her personality, can become submissive. It is a matter of the will and not the disposition. In fact, the disposition of a person can be very deceiving. I have known women with strong personalities who were very submissive to their husbands. On the other hand, I have known women who seemed to be meek and quiet who were in absolute domination over their husbands. Becoming submissive may not be understandable or even attractive to you as a wife, but if you would have a life of joy and happiness now and later, you must by faith take a stance of obedience to God and submission to your husband. Consider these steps in becoming submissive.

Step One: Acknowledging the Lordship of Christ

It is not likely that being a submissive wife will make any sense to you until Jesus Christ is the total Lord of your life. You will not understand the spirit of submission until you know the Submissive Savior as the ruler of your life. In him you find the most perfect combination of submission and authority. He was in authority with God and gave himself in submission to be the Redeemer of man. He submitted himself to death for us. If you are saved, this wonderful Christ lives *in* you! He in you is your hope of becoming everything as a wife that God ordained you to become. You are complete in him! (Col. 2:10).

In the light of this, why not take the declaration of lordship in your own life right now? If you need help in speaking with the Father, simply say, "Father, I will have this Jesus to rule over me. I believe that he lives in me, and I now assert and accept his total right to rule in every area of my life. I now, in Jesus name, submit to his lordship." He has been waiting for this moment and will be obliged to bring everything in your life under his scrutiny in order that he might make out of you everything you were made to become as a wife.

Step Two: Accepting Submission as a Gift of God

Submission has been defined as "the yielding of the power of authority to another." God has ordered the wife to be submissive to her husband, that is, to yield to his authority. This is her God-given role. God gives only good things. So many times he wants to give good things, but our logic tells us that the particular gift he wants to give is not good. So we refuse it and rebel against God and his order. Wife, don't try to figure out this matter of submission. Lead with your heart and receive the capacity of submission as a perfect gift from God. It may take a great deal of faith, but remember, "Without faith, it is impossible to please him" (Heb. 11:6). Reread the Scriptures relating to wifely submission in Ephesians 5:22–24; Colossians 3:18; 1 Peter 3:1–6; and Genesis 3:16. Accepting submission is a matter for the mind and emotions, as well as the will. The total consent of the first two may not come without the decisive action of the latter. The mind, though entertaining the thought, may not understand it. The emotions may be confused. But when the will decisively acts, God moves in to bring all the thoughts into captivity.

Consider saying something like this right now:

Lord, I believe that every good and every perfect gift is from above, and comes down from the Father of lights. I now receive the capacity for submission as a gift from you. I delight in it because I trust you completely. With it I receive your wisdom and power, resident in Christ who himself is resident within me, to proceed to become the wife that you have called me to be.

Step Three: Establishing Submission

The wife is not to wait until the husband begins to exhibit qualities that she deems worthy of her submission. Very often it works in just the opposite manner. Only when she by faith establishes her disposition of submission does he begin to manifest the qualities that have been there all along.

"Submission" is a noun. "Submit" is a verb and thus is an action. "Wives, submit," is the command of Ephesians 5:22. It is likely that this will take on action that is noticeable. It may need to be preceded by a confession to the husband that the wife has not been submissive as God's order has required. While submission is deeper than words, it is still important what we declare with our mouths. It may seem awkward, but a simple coronation may be in order in the establishing of the atmosphere of submission on the part of the wife. "Sarah obeyed Abraham, calling him lord; whose daughters are ye, as long as ye do well, and are not afraid with any amazement" (1 Pet. 3:6). It would not be sacrilege for the wife to call her husband "lord" for the meaning of it is simply "master."

The wife whose husband is not saved may be thinking at this point, "That will work for a wife whose husband is saved, but not for me." The Bible makes no distinction at this point. In fact in 1 Peter 3:1 the implication is that the husband who does not obey the Word will be won by the pure conduct of his wife. More husbands have been won by the purity of a wife's obedience than by the preaching of us all. A saved wife may shock an unsaved husband into considering his awesome responsibility of being the custodian of a home where lives are being shaped. As she announces that she is depending upon him as the head of the home, he begins to look for help. He will soon discover that there is no help apart from God and his Word. Paul has informed that "the unbelieving husband is sanctified by the wife" (1 Cor. 7:14). This does not mean that the husband can be saved "by proxy," but it does mean that a saved and obedient wife can be used as the means of setting the husband apart to be dealt with by the Lord. His chances of getting saved are greatly enhanced by having an obedient Christian for a wife.

So the command is the same. If your husband is an ideal husband to your way of thinking, "Wives, submit!" If your husband is a carnal Christian, and even in a state of rebellion against God, "Wives, submit." It is inevitable that the question be asked about obeying the husband in matters that counter Christian convictions. The answer cannot be put into a few words and could lead to an endless discussion of specific theoretical situations. It is well to say here that though the Bible states that the wife is to be in subjection "in everything" to her husband, there would be conditions imaginable where this would not be possible or advisable. I believe, however, that these would seldom occur (if ever) as God moved to bless the husband through his wife's submission. The subjection of a wife in dishonorable matters would not serve to bring a husband under conviction and bring him to Christ.

So wife, with faith in God, establish your submission to your husband just as you established your submission to Christ as Lord. You may even feel impressed to dramatize it by writing it out or speaking it or having a time of prayer with your husband in which you communicate it to God and your husband at the same time. Do not be alarmed if, even while you are doing it, there are sounds of protest coming from deep within you, but go on!

Implementing Submission

The *position* of submission having been *declared* the *disposition* of submission must now be *developed*. The wife will soon discover that the declaring of the position is much the easier of the two. Just as it was in salvation, so it will be in the matter of submission, "As ye have therefore received, so walk" (Col. 2:6).

Once the position has been taken, God is obliged to bring every thought of the mind into context with this new relationship. Every habit of life and the whole structure of the life-style will be brought under consideration. Many areas will immediately come to mind for investigation. Here are some of them:

> The discipline of the children
> The management of money matters
> The wife and extra family involvement
> The leadership in family worship
> Responsibility of teaching in the family
> Initiative in handling family problems
> Teaching submission to the children
> Implementing submission in little things

There will be times when it is helpful to remind each other of the new arrangement in a loving manner. Just as we need to continue to "reckon ourselves dead indeed unto sin" as Paul commanded in Romans 6:11, we need to reckon God's arrangement of submission continuously. The enterprising and innovative wife will find dozens of little ways to remind her husband that he is "lord" under the Lord Jesus. Just as God commands the establishing of submission he gloriously energizes for the carrying out of submission. The more impossible it seems to the wife the more obvious will be the release of the power of God into the situation giving the wife dynamic for submission.

Enjoying Submission

As difficult as submission is for some people, the joys of it in every case are more than compensating. Even in those cases where things seem to get worse instead of better, there is an inner peace making it all worthwhile. There are several facets that we begin immediately to enjoy upon submission. Here are some of them!

The joy of obedience to God's order.—When we obey the Lord, we discover that to a large measure obedience is its own reward. Obedience itself brings peace. We would need no other outward manifestation that we have done well. When we slip into the pattern of God for our lives, there is an unmistakable peace which floods the spirit of man and under the yoke of Christ there is a new kind of rest for the soul (Matt. 11:28–30).

The joy of meeting a husband's needs.—God planned for the wife's submission to meet the needs of her husband. She may have been taken up with her needs before, but now she finds joy in meeting needs through her God-ordained submission. And strangely enough she finds her own needs, long neglected, being met by the husband who responds favorably to her submissive spirit. Many a man, apparently weak, has been immediately strengthened by a wife's change of roles from independent to dependent. There is much in many a man waiting to come to life when his wife's submission begins to bring him to completion.

The joy of exemplifying the relationship between Christ and his church.—A submissive wife is the world's most adequate picture of the church, the Bride of Jesus Christ. As she submits to her husband, the completeness and cleansing which result, picture for the world the nature of the "true church."

The joy of a victorious atmosphere in the home.—An aura of peace abides in the atmosphere where God is pleased to dwell. The home where submission reigns (I like that!) is a place where the presence of God fills the very atmosphere. The devil is defeated by the very nature of the atmosphere. Have you ever walked into a home where there seemed to be oppression the moment you entered the door? It is more than imagination! Then you have had the pleasure of walking into a home where the secret of submission has been *employed* and is now being *enjoyed.*

The joy of viewing the kingdom and previewing heaven.—Would you know what the kingdom of God is like? Would you know the pleasures of eternity in heaven? You may get a view and a preview by having a home where God's order is established. Jesus reigns! There is peace.

These are only a few of the joys that will accompany the submission of one wife under God!

The Hint to Husbands . . . Love!

And now we come to the husband! You thought that we would never get there! There is much talk today about the submission of the wife. I have heard much less talk about the responsibility of the husband to love.

The command is quite simple; the implications are quite profound. "Husbands, love your wives, even *as* Christ also loved the church, and gave himself for it" (Eph. 5:25).

Headship . . . the Basis of Relationship

If the wife is to be submissive, there is a vital reason. The man to whom she is to be submissive is the "head" or the "headship." Before we move into the matter of husbands and their responsibility to love their wives, let us establish a perspective from which he is to do it. Here is the basic statement: "For the husband is the head of the wife, even *as* Christ is the head of the church" (Eph. 5:23). Husband, get acquainted with the simple, but mighty little word "as!" It is so important that if you miss it, you will miss the whole foundation upon which your marriage is structured. You are the head! This is a position that God has ordained. That does not mean that you are superior or that you have the right to be a dictator over your wife. Neither does it mean that you can demand her to be your servant. (You will find that your position as head will mean just the opposite!) Neither does your headship mean that you have the right to treat your wife just anyway you get ready to treat her. In fact, because you are the head that puts you directly in line in responsibility to God who is *your* head.

Be sure that how you treat the one who looks to you as head will greatly affect the relationship between you and the One to whom you look as Head. (Read this statement again!) *The Living Bible* has an interesting paraphrase of 1 Peter 3:7: "You husbands must be careful of your wives, being thoughtful of their needs and honoring them as the weaker sex. Remember that you and your wife are partners in receiving God's blessings, and if you don't treat her as you should, your prayers will not get ready answers."

As shocking as it may seem, the problem with the husband's headship is sometimes more of a problem with the husband than with the wife. Husband, be it known to you that it is not a matter of option for you in this matter of authority. Whether you feel like taking authority or headship or not . . . you are the head. You must not succumb to either pitfall of refusing the position or abusing the position. Either is catastrophic.

The little word "as" is your key! The husband is head of the wife "as" Christ is head of the church. Christ has been given headship because of who he is and what he has done! He has died for the church and now, having died, he lives for the church as the divine indweller and the divine intercessor. Headship on the part of the husband, then, is loving availability and loving leadership. The home that is in God's proper order is the perfect visual aid portraying the relationship between Christ and his church. Christ is the head of the church. As he is recognized head, his person and power can be truly reflected and those under his authority will gain the maximum of benefits. Likewise, the husband, as he is the recognized head of the home is able to be all that God intended him to be in terms of benefit to the wife and family. Thus, you have the precise reason for this whole discourse.

The Meaning of That Love

While we could give a technical definition of love from the psychological viewpoint, it seems more helpful to give a list of the action of love, both negative and positive. The husband is commanded to love his wife. First Corinthians 13 indicates to us in clear terms the love that is from God . . . *agape* love. Husband, check your deportment against the following list. If you are doing what love is doing and not doing what love is not doing, there is a good chance that you are loving.

LOVE DOES . . .
> endure long, acts kindly, and rejoices in the truth.

LOVE DOES NOT . . .
> envy, get proud or puffed up.

LOVE DOES NOT . . .
> behave rudely (unmannerly), seek its own, get easily provoked, or think evil.

LOVE DOES NOT . . .
> rejoice in iniquity or injustice.

LOVE DOES . . .
> bear all things, believe all things, hope all things, and endure all things (1 Cor. 13:4,6).

By the way, there is one more characteristic of love . . . IT NEVER FAILS!

Now, husband, let me make a request of you. If you really want to check yourself, look back across what love does and what love does not do and put in the place of the word "love" the words "a godly husband." YOU! After you have done that, do one other thing. Put your name in the place of "godly husband" and read through the list once again. How does it fit? "Ouch," you say? But listen, if you can make it through all the "does" and "does nots," look at what you have at the end. Love never fails! A godly husband never fails! You, loving as you should, never fail!

Now you have surveyed the meaning of love as evidenced in its actions both positive and negative. I am sorry, but you cannot grade yourself and pass. You either make 100 percent or fail! Love does not *sometimes* do this or that! It *always* does what it does. Love does not *sometimes* refrain from a course of actions. It *always* does not do what it does not do. What am I saying? Precisely this . . . "You either love or you do not!" Are you bewildered! Good! To find out how to love as you are commanded, to love as a husband, keep on reading.

The Measure of That Love

I have warned you about that little word that is a lightweight in sound, but in reality is profound . . . "as." This is the word that can take a *known*, link it to an *unknown*, and make it as *known* as the former. "As Christ loved the church" is a *known;* "How a husband should love his wife is an *unknown*. Link them together with the little word "as" and you have two *knowns*.

Thus, the first word regarding the measure of the love of the husband for the wife is "as Christ loved the church." How did Christ love the church?

First, he loved it *selflessly*. That is, he gave himself for it. He made himself available to it. He did not regard his estate prior to the incarnation too much to give up for his future body and bride, the church. His every action was selfless. He did what he did for us and not for himself. The husband is to love the wife in the same manner. He is to count nothing too precious to give up on her account.

Jesus Christ the Lord not only gave himself to be available for the church, but to die for the church. Thus, he loved the church *sacrificially.* He sacrificed himself for his church! The husband's typical response may be, "Why, I would be willing to die for my wife!" The issue is not willingness. Jesus was more than willing to die for the church. He did die! The husband who loves his wife as Christ loved the church likewise will die. He will die to his individuality, his likes, his preferences, his plans as a single man, his ideas, and his opinions. In fact, before there can be a proper marriage, there must of necessity be a "double funeral." Two people must die to their individuality and to their ideas of thinking as individuals in order to live to one another.

A few years ago a missionary and his wife were having quite a struggle both on the mission field and in their personal lives. In a series of spiritual life conferences they squarely faced the issues in their relationship with God and came through to glorious victory. I was there when it happened. I never saw such confession. First, they confessed to God and then to each other. Tears flowed and with the flowing tears, resentments were washed away. Their whole lives were changed. Later, in describing to friends what happened, they reported, "We had two funerals and a wedding!" Many a home would be much blessed by two such "funerals."

Not only is the husband to love his wife as Christ loved the church, but he is to love her *as he loves his own body.* This, too, characterizes the measure of his love for her. There is something sick about a man who will do harm to his own body. Psychologists have a name for such a man. I have a name for such a man. He is sick, silly, and stupid! A normal man cares for his body. He rests it, nourishes it with food, gives it medicine when it is sick, and gives it exercise. He dresses it for comfort and seeks to create conditions as ideal for its maximum welfare as possible. "So ought men to love their wives as their own bodies. He that loveth his wife loveth himself. For no man ever yet hated his own flesh; But nourisheth and cherisheth it, even as the Lord the church" (Eph. 5:28–29).

The Bible encourages healthy and wholesome self-love. We are exhorted to love each other as we love ourselves. He that loves his wife is loving himself. She is a part of himself. She is the rest of him!

Husband, love your wife as Christ loved the church and as you love your own body and as you love yourself.

The Motive of That Love

The influence of the little word "as" lives on! If the husband is to love his wife as Christ loved the church, he will love her for the same motive and the same results will endue. In verse 26 the "that" introduces the motive of love. Christ loved the church that he might sanctify and cleanse it with the washing of water by the word." Christ's love for the church set it apart as his very own property and cleansed it. Love has a "setting apart" power as well as a cleansing power. All this is with a view to union. Love seeks union. A lover's happiness is consummated in union with the loved. The love of Christ was his "givingness" with a view to union. The lover does not see his happiness in terms of himself, but in terms of his beloved. Christ died for us that we might be united with him forever. Therefore the ultimate motive in this love (both of the Christ and the husband) is "that he might present it to himself a glorious church, not having spot, or wrinkle, or any such thing" (v. 27).

Husband, have you ever suspicioned that if your wife is not what you think she ought to be, it might be your fault. You see, it is your love that releases the sanctifying power of Christ in her life. You are to love her "as" (in the manner as, just like, with the same love as) Christ loved the church. Just as Christ's love was the enabling power for the church to become what she should be, the love of the husband is the dynamic needed to make the wife what she should be.

The Manner of That Love

Do you begin to see the thickening plot? Marriage is God's great frame-up to make us what we ought to be! Husband, you are to love your way to wholeness. "But how?" is the dilemma. Any man, after facing the issue, desires to do what God tells him to do! But how can he do it? I have both bad news and good news. The bad news is "he can't!" The good news is "he can!"

Let's take the bad news first. No man can love anybody (especially his wife) as Christ loved the Church. He does not have it in him as a man. He is totally incapable in himself of producing any good thing. You must believe that! As long as you are unconvinced, you will try to produce love and you will continue to be a miserable failure. The longer you try, the greater will be the resulting tragedy. That is the bad news!

The good news? "He can!" Jesus can love your wife through you! You say, "But he's not me and I am not he! If you are truly saved, really born again, you have no right to say that! When you were redeemed by the blood of Christ, you received him into your life. You never have the right again to think of yourself as being apart from him. You two (Christ and you) have become one. He is in you and you are in him. In fact, 1 John 4:17 says, "As he is, so are we in this world." Here is the good news. *Christ in you, in control of you, can love your wife as he loved the church.* Paul said, "I am crucified with Christ: nevertheless I live; yet not I, but Christ liveth in me: and the life which I now live in the flesh, I live by the faith of the Son of God, who loved me, and gave himself for me" (Gal. 2:20).

Husband, here is your key . . . *Yet not I, but Christ liveth in me.* Christ lives in you to live victoriously and to love victoriously. We are informed that the fruit of the Spirit is *love.* That is, when the Spirit of Christ is in control of us, we will love. This is the only manner in which it can be done. Husbands, love your wives!

The summation of this rather lengthy chapter is simply this:

Wives, *submit* your way to victory!

Husbands, *love* your way to victory!

Yours will be the joy of . . .

"One home under God!"

You see, the whole idea was God's. He made Adam to be the bridegroom and Eve to be the bride and the wife. He performed the first marriage while the birds sang and the animals gazed in wonder. God inaugurated the first home, and gave to each member of the family his own unique responsibility. How natural it is, then, to look to God and to the Word of God for wise instructions concerning the happiness of the home and the delineation of the duties of its members. Actually, it narrows down to this: **successful husbands are those who follow God's directives.** Husbands are failures when they ignore his wisdom.

WILLIAM W. ORR

4 The Pattern for Husbands

We have observed in the last chapter that the role of Christ as the head of the Church was to be the guideline for the role of the husband in the home. The husband is to love his wife as Christ loved the church. We looked at the meaning, measure, motive, and manner of that love. True love will thrust us into roles that we may not even have known to exist. In this chapter I want to observe with you the roles that confront every husband. As he fills, under God, these roles in Christ-controlled fashion, the results will be marvelous. Again we will use the little word "as" to connect the ministry of Jesus as the bridegroom of the church and the ministry of the husband as head of the wife.

The Husband as Provider

As Christ in his death for the church provided and in his life continues to provide for his own, the husband indwelt with Christ will do the same. He is, to his wife, the embodiment of all that Christ was to the church. The wife and family are uniquely the husband's responsibility. Our society today has little problem realizing a part of this. But there seems to be some massive blind spots in our vision at this point. The obvious point at which our society would say "Amen" would be at the point of provision for the physical necessities. We probably do not need to say much about this as it is generally accepted. The Word does make clear the severity of the failure to provide. "But if any provide not for his own, and specially for those of his own house, he hath denied the faith, and is worse than an infidel" (1 Tim. 5:8).

It would be difficult to imagine any infraction more severe than this. Almost any law-abiding citizen would be in accord with this declaration from the Scriptures. It may be fearful, however, to know what all this verse does include as far as provision is concerned. The husband's provision is to include far more than food, clothing, and shelter.

The husband is to provide *identity*. When the husband and wife stood at the marriage altar, they became "Mr. and Mrs." She took his name. She left the name of her birth and took the name of his birth. What a responsibility he has! The children will have his name. He will be the source of their identity. He will bring them up to the level of his name or lower them to the level of it. Just as we are purchased to be conformed to the image of God's Son so the family will take on the likenesses of the head of the home. This will include the physical, mental, moral, and spiritual. Husband, you cannot escape it. You will give your family an identity. It may be good. It may be bad. It cannot be avoided!

The husband is to provide *unity*. The church is the church of the Lord Jesus Christ. He is the center around which all the church gathers. Paul affirms that "by him all things consist" (Col. 1:17). The husband is the "stack pole" of family life. He is to provide its center. The word "husband" means "house band." He is the band which holds the house together.

The husband is to provide *destiny*. He sets the direction of the family. Without him there is no sense of direction or destiny. Just as Jesus could say to his own, "Follow me!" so should the husband have such direction in his own life as to be able to say to his family, "Follow me." We will see that this destiny includes every area of the life of the family. What the husband is plays as important a role as what he says in setting the destiny of the family.

So we see that the husband as provider furnishes *security, identity, unity,* and *destiny*. Christ has provided all this for the church.

The Husband as Protector

The husband has died to single life to become the headship of a home. He now lives to protect that which his death has purchased. His obligation to protect is as great as his obligation to provide. The animal world recognizes this as a basic drive.

The husband is to protect his wife and family *physically.* He is to stand between them and possible physical harm.

The husband is to protect his wife and family *socially.* He is to absorb the pressures in social circumstances in himself instead of leaving the family unprotected.

The husband is to protect his wife and family *spiritually.* He has the unique position of standing between his family and the powers of darkness. The devil is forced to recognize the authority of the husband and father in the home. That protection is to be internal as well as external. To protect against the attacks of the devil without building the superstructure of a spiritual life for all members of his family is work without wisdom.

The husband is to protect his wife and family *mentally* and *emotionally.* He is the guardian of the trust of truth. We shall see later that he is more than just guardian. In protection of the truth he will stand against that which is not true in its invasion of the home. His authority properly exercised will mean a protection from mental attitudes which cause serious emotional traumas later on. It is a fact without argument that homes where God's order is in progress are homes where there is little emotional and mental illness.

A husband who is filled with the Spirit of Christ will, by his very presence, create a protective atmosphere in the home. All that is not of the will of God will be repelled by this unseen protection. Jesus Christ lives today to protect his own interests. He died to redeem us as his bride and he lives to retain us so that he might present us to himself perfect! The husband, committed to the wife at the marriage altar, now remains available to be her protector.

The Husband as Priest

While it is true that every member of the body of Christ is a priest unto God, the husband has a unique role as the priest of the family. This does not mean that the wife and children cannot come to God on their own. It does mean that as they come unto God, they can come under the protection of the husband and father. It also means that he has the unique privilege of coming to God in behalf of his family. He ministers at the altar in their behalf. A priest is a representative for someone else. He makes pleas on their behalf and makes himself available to God for the meeting of those needs.

The greatest role of the priest is that of intercession. If every father could awaken to the ministry of intercession on behalf of the children God has given him, the lives of those children would be different. If every husband were to awaken to the power of his intercession in behalf of his wife, he would be found praying for her much more and there would be miracles occurring in their relationship. May I share with you some of the patterns into which God has led me in praying for my family? This has been of great comfort to me and I believe of great benefit for the future as well as the present.

I have before me my prayer notebook. In that notebook I have the names of many people for whom I pray. After the pages of praise, there is a page for each member of my family. I mark the date of the prayer, the specific prayer Scripture, and anything else that the Lord leads me to put down. Let me take some of those entries out of the prayer notebook to give you an idea of how I pray for my family:

The date was 5–14–73. The Scripture I felt impressed to pray for my son, Timothy, was from the book by that name. My prayer was something like this, "I pray that Tim, according to the prophecies which went before him, might war a good warfare" (1 Tim. 1:18–19). On the same day I prayed for my son according to 2 Timothy 3:14–17. "I pray that Tim will continue in the things which he has seen and heard and be wise unto salvation through faith which is in Christ Jesus. I pray that the Word may be profitable for Tim in doctrine, reproof, correction, and instruction in righteousness that Tim may be, as a man of God, thoroughly furnished unto all good work."

As Timmy's intercessor, I know that if I ask anything according to the will of God, God hears. I further know that if God hears what

I pray according to his will, I have already received what I asked of him (1 John 5:14–15). This is precisely why I love to pray the Scriptures. I am simply giving back to God in prayer what he gave to me in the Bible. There is a wealth of material on praying for each other all through the Bible.

As I pray for my children, I am aware that just as the prayers of Jesus for his own are still being answered, my prayers for my own will go on being answered down through the years of time. I can pray for my children's vocational adjustment, future education, future husband or wife, and opportunities for service to God. I can wrap them in a glorious network of prayer that will clothe them to walk in places of physical, emotional, moral, and spiritual danger.

I feel very definite about my role as the praying priest for my family. This does not alleviate them from their need to pray or from my need to pray with them. My task to pray *for* them, however, is supreme.

As I pray for my son on another occasion, I may pray the entire First Psalm for him. "Blessed is Tim who walks not in the counsel of the ungodly, nor stands in the way of sinners, nor sits in the seat of the scornful. But Tim's delight shall be in the law of the Lord, and in his law will Tim meditate day and night. Tim shall be like a tree planted by the rivers of waters, that brings forth his fruit in his season; his leaf shall not wither; and whatsoever Tim does will prosper. The Lord knows Tim's way."

As I pray for my daughter, Tammy, I may pray the whole thirty-first chapter of Proverbs for her, claiming that she will be the kind of woman portrayed in this chapter. On 5–15–72 I prayed this for Tammy, "And the very God of peace sanctify Tammy wholly; and I pray God Tammy's whole spirit, soul, and body be preserved blameless unto the coming of the Lord Jesus Christ. "Faithful is he that calls her, who will also do it!" This is 1 Thessalonians 5:23–24. On another day I prayed that she, like Jehoshaphat of old, may have a heart to seek the Lord as he is recorded having done in 2 Chronicles 20 when told of an enemy invasion.

Over both my children I simply pray back to God the promises he has made to them. "My God is now supplying all Timmy's and Tammy's needs according to his riches in glory by Christ Jesus" (see

Phil. 4:19). How rich the Scriptures are in the realm of our priesthood as we pray for each other!

I declare in prayer that "Jesus is made unto my family, wisdom, and righteousness, and sanctification, and redemption" (1 Cor. 1:30).

As I pray for my wife I recite such verses as Colossians 1:9–11: "I desire that Barbara might be filled with the knowledge of God's will in all wisdom and spiritual understanding; that she might walk worthy of the Lord unto all pleasing, being faithful in every good work, and increasing in the knowledge of God; that Barbara might be strengthened, according to his glorious power, unto all patience and longsuffering with joyfulness." Another verse that I have prayed for my wife is 2 Thessalonians 3:5. "I pray that the Lord will direct Barbara's heart into the love of God, and into the patient waiting for Christ."

Now, do you begin to see what the priesthood of the husband and father can involve? It involves the delightful privilege of discovering the will of God for our families within the pages of the Word of God. It also involves praying these Scriptures into reality in the lives of the members of my family. It further involves giving to them an inheritance which no one on the face of the earth can take away from them . . . the heritage of prayers prayed for them which will be answered as the time comes for the will of God to be carried out in their lives.

If taking time to earn a living, which puts food on the table, clothes on their backs, and a shelter for them is worthy, of how much more worth is it to take time to pray for the family. In prayer we transact divine business which hedges our children in to the will of God all the days of their lives. God help us to take our priesthood seriously.

The Husband as Prophet

A priest is one who goes before God in behalf of someone else. A prophet is someone who goes to someone in behalf of God. The husband is not only priest, but prophet. He "forthtells" the Word of God to his family. He exhorts according to the Word. Having gone to God in their behalf, he now comes to them on God's behalf to share with them what he has learned in the study and the prayer closet. Impressions should come through the Word which he can share with his family. Every home should have a "resident" prophet as the head of the house!

The Husband as Professor

Not only should the husband tell forth the Word of God to his family, but he should be resident professor in his home. This does not mean that there will be formal classes (though that might not be a bad idea) but it means that at every opportunity he will teach the truth of which he has become a guardian. The home is the classroom where more is learned than anywhere in the child's environment. This is where we should have our best teachers. I am much afraid that we are allowing our children to be taught by implication more violence than victory in Christ, more pollution than purity, more immorality than integrity. This comes chiefly through the means of the television set. The years have gone that found us protesting against filthy movies in the theatres of our towns. These same movies now are coming into our homes through the television. It is nothing for the average American family to sit quietly and reverently before the television set for twenty hours per week! How much could be done in half that amount of time in teaching of the integrity of labor, the sanctity of sex, and the nobility of selflessness. Husband, you are the professor. You set the curriculum, you teach the classes, and you eventually will see the result of your teachings both good and bad! You should be the professor of economics, sex education, sociology, religion, and history.

The Husband as Partner

The husband is to be all of the preceding as well as *partner.* "Remember that you and your wife are *partners* in receiving God's blessings . . ." (1 Pet. 3:7*b*, TLB). The term used in the Authorized Version is "heirs together of the grace of life." The action of the husband and wife should be consistent with this partnership. Otherwise the prayers of the husband may not get ready answers (1 Pet. 3:7*c*). Partners in business are not free to view the business from a single viewpoint. Their attitude toward each other is one of concern because they realize that whatever affects the partner affects the business. So with the marriage partnership. Sorrows are shared in togetherness, blessings are received in togetherness, problems are considered in togetherness, and profits are accepted in togetherness.

What a glorious partnership is shared in the marriage relationship! Here are partners who have submitted their lives to each other unconditionally and permanently. All that is faced will be faced *together*. What a wonderful word . . . together! How pleasant is that word regardless of circumstances. I remember when my wife and I faced the loss of our first child. We had shared the anticipations of his coming, *together*. He lived three days. I watched him live out the last moments of his earthly life. We shared the sorrow of his going, *together*. I could not bear to think of what it might have been had there not been the privilege of sharing it *together*.

We are *partners together!*

The Husband as Pal

"Let's be friends!" It would be surprising what would happen in homes across America if members of the family could agree on that declaration. The tragedy of most homes is that husband and wife are not true friends to each other. They are not as friendly with each other as with other friends. They do not share things in common as friends do. In fact, if most husbands and wives treated their friends as they do each other, they would probably not have any friends in thirty days!

One of the most enjoyable results of the miracle in our home is that my wife is my best friend and I am hers! I can be an adequate provider, an able provider,

an apt priest,

an alert prophet,

and an astute professor . . .

but if I am not a partner and a friend or pal much of the good may be lost.

I have discovered that my family are my friends. My daughter is my best female friend next to my wife. We sometimes go out, just she and I. I enjoy her as a good friend. My son is my best male friend. Yes, there is a generation gap! There always has been and always will be. God ordained it and he also ordained *authority* and *love* as the two-lane highway across the gap. The father can be friends with his son and/or daughter without compromising his position.

Let's take time to make friends! Let us say of our mates what Solomon's wife said of him, "This is my beloved and this is my *friend*" (Song of Solomon 5:16).

What I have been saying is that the role of the husband is a serious role indeed. It involves his being, to the glory of God, a *provider,* a *protector,* a *priest,* a *prophet,* a *professor,* a *partner,* and a *pal* for and to his wife and family. As you discover your roles under God you will have "one home under God."

The most influential position in the nation today is held by a woman. She enforces law, practices medicine, and teaches . . . without a degree, certificate of competence, or required training. She handles the nation's food, administers its drugs, and practices emergency first aid. This for the spiritual, physical, and mental ills of the American family. A man literally places his life and the lives of his children in the hands of this woman . . . HIS WIFE.

RUTH HAMPTON

5 The Pattern for Wives

> Divine order always assures happiness; there is
> no godly or spiritual woman who would want it
> changed.—*McClaren*

There is no higher calling than that of being a wife and mother.
In his book, *Love Happily Ever After,* David Seamands shares a story
about Uncle Buddy Robinson, the famous camp meeting preacher.
A woman was converted under his ministry and a few days later came
to him and said that she felt that God was calling her to preach. Uncle
Bud asked her if she had any children. To this she replied, "Oh, yes,
I have a very large family," and his face lit up. With that inimitable
lisp of his, he said, "Well, bless God, Sister, God's not only called
you to preach, He's given you a congregation as well!" This is a
theological fact. Every wife and mother has been provided a congregation and a sanctuary . . . her children and the home!

We have observed the central response of the wife to her husband
to be submissive. The quality of this submission is to be measured by
the little word "as." "Therefore as the church is subject unto Christ,
so let the wives be to their own husbands in every thing" (Eph. 5:24).
Just as we find the key for the pattern of the husband within the
context of the relationship of Christ to his church, we discover the
key to the wife's pattern in the church's relationship to Christ. Let

61

us look briefly at the implications of this relationship. The husband is provider, protector, priest, prophet, professor, partner, and pal. In order for him to function to the limit of his intentions there is the necessity that the wife recognize these roles and joyfully receive the ministry of her husband. Wife, it would be well to ask yourself how you stand in relationship with your husband in each of these capacities. Is there one or more of these about which you seem to have a driving compulsion to "take over"?

The church should be "filled with gratitude" for its head, the Lord Jesus. God has set the husband over the wife to guard his precious interests. The husband is an integral part of God's redemptive scheme. As the church looks toward Christ with gratitude for his redeeming qualities, the wife is to look toward her husband for his redeeming qualities. He is to her the means of living to the fullest the purposes of God in this life.

The church should "reverence" (respect) the Lord Jesus. She is to worship, adore, and exalt him. There are features of all these three in the wife's attitude toward her husband. She is to reverence him, that is, respect him with total trust (Eph. 5:33).

The *desires* of the church are toward Christ. Christ is all, therefore, the body of Christ will find its total provision in him. All the desires of the body are toward the head. God spoke to the woman after the fall and said, "Thy desire shall be to thy husband" (Gen. 3:16). As the wife trusts her desire to her husband she will discover that he will more completely fulfill her desires than she herself. The bride of Christ has eyes for no one else but him. She is exclusively his. She longs to see him, waits for his coming with great expectation, and desires to be exactingly loyal to him. The wife longs for the sight of, enjoys the presence of, and waits for the direction of her husband.

The church is *available* to the Lord Jesus. The church is the means of giving Christ expression. She is to reflect his love and character. He dwells in his body in order to move about in this world and get his work done. The wife is to have the same availability to her husband. She is delighted with this availability because she knows that as she becomes available to her husband, he becomes available to her. Mutual submission leads to mutual availability. "No man ever hated his own flesh; but nourisheth and cherisheth it, even as the Lord the church" (Eph. 5:28). If the wife will be as available to her husband as the body is to the head, he will be inclined to treat her as his body with respect and provision in joy.

The church *cherishes fellowship* with the risen Lord. There is the fellowship of *worship* as well as the fellowship of *service*. The wife delights in the fellowship with her husband and recognizes that her highest privileges are found in that fellowship. The deep spiritual significance of sex speaks of the fellowship between Christ and his church. There is deep expression, communication, and satisfaction in this fellowship.

The quality and quantity of this relationship are total . . . "in everything" (Eph. 5:24*b*). As these patterns are fulfilled, God is able to bring the scheme of heaven down to earth. As we pray, "Thy kingdom come, thy will be done on earth as it is in heaven," we are praying for the patterns of heaven in the home.

What Manner of Woman

"The man who finds a wife, finds a good thing; she is a blessing to him from the Lord" (Prov. 18:22, TLB). King Lemuel echoes that in Proverbs 31 and gives us the most comprehensive description of a great wife to be found in the Bible. "If you can find a truly good wife, she is worth more than precious gems" (Prov. 31:10). Here is God's standard for the godly wife:

Her husband can trust her and she satisfies his needs (vv. 11–12).

She is industrious, energetic, frugal, and wise (vv. 14–18).

She has a heart for the poor and needy (vv. 19–20).

She provides for the needs of her family and prepares for the eventualities of harder times (vv. 21–22).

She is such a wife that her husband is freed to fulfill an important role in public life (v. 23).

She is a woman of her word and kind as well (v. 25).

She is not lazy or idle (v. 27).

Her children bless her and her husband praises her (v. 28).

Would you have your husband say, "There are many fine women in the world, but you are the best of them all"? Then allow God to make you like the woman of Proverbs 31!

If we consented to the wisdom of having patron saints, surely Sarah would be the patron saint of wives. First Peter further clarifies the pattern of the wife's conduct and character in First Peter 3. A pure conduct is to be coupled with a reverent spirit. A meek and a quiet spirit is of great price in the sight of God. Sarah was this kind of a woman. She fitted into her husband's plans. Can you imagine what it took to simply go along with Abraham when he heard from the Lord regarding leaving the security of Ur of the Chaldees? She was willing to follow him as he followed the Lord. She called him "lord." Such a woman need not be afraid. Lord, increase the number of the "daughters of Sarah!"

The Covered Woman

The issue of the role of women in the church is a vital one. It was vital enough when Paul was writing to occupy a part of the first Corinthian letter. The woman may serve, pray, or prophesy as long as her head is covered. What sort of strange ritual would make this a necessity? The covering of a woman's head in those days was a symbol of her recognition of the headship of her husband under God. Her true covering was her husband. His headship was God. The woman is to have liberty to minister under the authority of her husband. As long as she operates within this context, she is over whatever is under him.

There are two classes of women mentioned here . . . the covered woman and the uncovered woman. A piece of cloth or covering cannot make a woman godly or render her godless. However, her recognition of her position and the submissive acceptance of it quickly categorizes her as a godly woman ready for service. Such a woman, protected by God's authority, knows when to speak and when to pray. She will not be frustrated and her service will not be frustrating to others. She is strong, but not dominating!

Luther said of his wife, "The greatest gift of God is a pious, amiable spouse, who fears God, loves his house, with whom one can live in perfect confidence."

The wife of General Booth was such a woman. When the founder of the Salvation Army was still in the Wesleyan ministry, a crisis arose. He felt the call to evangelism. The conference voted against his giving full time to the work of evangelism. It was for William Booth a great crisis. If he went against the vote, he would have to leave the Wesleyan ministry. His income would be no more. His home and future would be threatened. He hesitated and was urged to agree with the vote of the conference. There was a pause in the meeting and the air was filled with tenseness. Suddenly, a female voice was heard shouting from the gallery, "William, never!" A woman had risen to her feet and dared to cry, "Never!" It was the wife of William Booth. He took courage from the challenge and stood firm with the call of God. It was the beginning of the Salvation Army. It was no wonder at her funeral that her husband described her as "A tree who had shadowed him from the burning sun, whose flower had been the adornment and beauty of his life, whose fruit had been the stay of his existence . . . a servant who had served without fee or reward . . . a counselor who had advised, and seldom advised wrong . . . a friend who had understood his very nature . . . a wife who for forty years had never given him cause for grief . . . who had ever been the strongest when the battle was the strongest. She was the delight of his eyes and the inspiration of his soul. She was good . . . she was love . . . she was a spiritual warrior."

Shakespeare wrote of sleep and described the godly wife:

> She must knit together the raveled sleeve of care.
> She is sore labor's bath, balm of hurt minds,
>   Chief nourisher in life's feast.
> She is like a holy oil giving light and nourishment,
>   And warmth to those within her home,
> And to the wandering child, she is like a candle that's
>   Set in a window at night.

Jesus lives and works in the life of an obedient child. An obedient child therefore is a happy child. The child who knows exactly how far he can go is relieved of a heavy burden.

LARRY CHRISTENSON

6 The Pattern for Children

Children may be described as the crowning unity of
the home.

We look two directions in this chapter . . . toward the child from
the view of the parent and toward the parent from the view of the
child. The heart of our problem as far as the manifestation is concerned is found in this area. While the real problems may be deeper,
the first visible sighting of problems may be in the responses of children to their parents.

A recently released study conducted by the National Industrial
Conference suggested that by 1980 three out of every five families
would have a child living at home. To put it another way, the nation's
parent population is expected to increase by 23 percent during the
1970's, faster than any comparable period since World War II. Not
only will more people be parents, but the parents of the years ahead
will be younger, more affluent, and better schooled than parents of
the past.

We are all children and most people who read these lines have living
parents. Before going to the subject of parents and children living
together in homes, I want to remark of our responsibilities as continuing children. At marriage, family ties are broken. We remove ourselves from the premises of our old home and begin to make a new

one. We are no longer subject to Father and Mother to obey them as before. We are not, however, released from all responsibility to them. The first commandment with promise is, "Honour thy father and mother" (Eph. 6:2). The promise is, "That thy days may be long upon the land . . ." (Ex. 20:12). While we may no longer be obliged to obey our parents, we are never exempt from honoring them. One of the sins of our age is the dishonoring of parents. It is possible to dishonor parents and not live with them. May I ask you some pertinent questions at this point that I am reminded to often ask myself? (This is for those with at least one living parent.)

In what ways are you honoring your father and mother?

How long has it been since a letter conveyed your interest and concern?

Do you remember them on their birthdays, anniversaries, and other special days?

How long has it been since you called them on the telephone and just had conversation with them?

Would you look forward to being given the same concern by your children that you are giving your parents?

How long has it been since you simply enumerated to them the reasons for your deep appreciation of them?

I am forever coming to new values in life simply because of the upbringing in my home. My parents taught much without making the surroundings seem like a classroom. I am not even sure that they knew that they were teaching, but they were just being honest, godly, and law-abiding folks. They believed in old-fashioned values and their conduct so perfectly supported their convictions that the validity of these could not be denied. Every now and then I am brought to a new sense of gratitude for God giving me my parents. I tell the Lord about it, but that does not seem to be enough. My parents need to know. They have made an investment of time, money, and life. It is only fitting that the interest on the investment be theirs.

Why don't you just resolve right now that you will deliberately upgrade your relationship with your parents? God will honor it, you will enjoy it, and they will be blessed.

From Parent to Child

Our children are new expressions of the glory of the unity of marriage. We have done something together that could not have been done alone. As a result of mutual submission, mutual affection, and the deepest intimacies of love, God has given us children. We have shared in the creation of another life. That life will be an exact reproduction of all the conduct, character, and responses of his parents. There will be computed into his brain all the words he hears, all the scenes of conflict that he sees, and all the love, fears, hate, or rejection that he feels.

Love for the children is not demanded on the part of the parents . . . it is assumed. Built within the human frame is a love for our own that is as clear a type of the love the Father has for his children everywhere. We are not told to love our children. It is needless to tell us. If we know Christ, it is inevitable.

The clearest indication of love is discipline. Within parent-love there is affection and acceptance, but real love always goes beyond this. In his book, *Christian Dimensions in Family Living,* Kemp gives the four basic needs of children as:

AFFECTION

ACCEPTANCE

ATTENTION

ACHIEVEMENT

Love will provide all of these and discipline as well. Look at the repeated exhortation from God's Word to discipline.

"If you refuse to discipline your son, it proves you don't love him; for if you love him, you will be prompt to punish him" (Prov. 13:25, TLB).

"A youngster's heart is filled with rebellion, but punishment will drive it out of him" (Prov. 22:15, TLB).

"Don't fail to correct your children, discipline won't hurt them! They won't die if you use a stick on them! Punishment will keep them out of hell!" (Prov. 23:13–14, TLB)

"Scolding and spanking a child helps him to learn. Left to himself, he brings shame to his mother" (Prov. 29:15, TLB).

"Discipline your son and he will give you happiness and peace of mind" (Prov. 29:17, TLB).

"And ye fathers, provoke not your children to wrath; but bring them up in the nurture and admonition of the Lord" (Eph. 6:4).

Discipline does not stop with punishment. It is never an end in itself. It is a means to bring direction toward integrity and character. In Ephesians 6:4 the two areas of influence are "nurture" and "admonition." The first literally means "child training" and the latter means "a putting in mind." The first is done in training by actions; the latter, in training by words. One is incomplete without the other. If actions and words do not correspond, a confused child is the end result.

Parents, yours is a serious vocation. If you shirk it, the expense will be high and will continue for generations. To do the job as it should be done will take more than your money, your time, and your planning. It will take *you!* It will take you . . . totally involved and totally available . . . not only to your family, but to God. It is not a job you can do by yourself. You cannot love without God in the manner which the task requires.

In proper patterns within the home, the child will be the benefactor of the flow of divine life according to God's order. When authority is as it should be, God is pleased to move, bless, and dwell where it is happening. As this happens all will become aware of God's love and abundant life. Every promise in the Word of God is not only a personal promise, but a promise for the family. Jesus said, "I am come that they might have life and that they might have it more abundantly" (John 10:10). This is for your family and mine!

From Child to Parent

I have read through dozens of books on the subject of the family. I have discovered that there is very little material written to the child regarding his responsibilities. I see several reasons for this situation. First, not many children are going to read the books. Second, the simplicity of the biblical pattern of the child in the home leaves little room for discussion. "Children, obey your parents in the Lord; for this is right" (Eph. 6:1). That is simply it!

The reason for it is just as simple. "That it may be well with thee, and thou mayest live long on the earth" (Eph. 6:2). At this writing my wife and I are the parents of two teenagers, Tammy and Timmy. You have heard from them briefly in refrains from an earlier chapter. I would like for you to hear from them again as I simply ask them some questions and allow them to respond from the "teener's point of view." I am happy to tell you that when God began to do a deeper work in our home, our children became a treasure to us in ways that we had never thought were possible. We discovered in them valuable points of view that aided us in vital decisions, strengthened us in crises, and supported us in matters requiring unshaken faith. Listen to Tammy and Timmy:

Question: What do you believe that teenagers really want in the family relationship?

TAMMY: They want closeness to their parents and the privilege of talking to them without feeling intimidated. They want to have fun with their parents. They want to be trusted and to be given responsibility.

TIMMY: They want love. Some parents are gone from their children most of the time and feel that they can provide things and that will be enough. Some children would feel glad to get a kick in the pants from their parents. This would at least be some attention and a sign of love. They want a family and that means closeness.

Question: From your view as a teenager what is the greatest need in family life today?

TAMMY: Communication! This begins with communication with God and then through the family. Communication takes time and effort on the part of everyone. Dad should take the lead and when he doesn't, Mom should. Communication leads to respect and love.

TIMMY: A real relationship with God as a family. This means that each one must have his very own relationship with God. When God and Jesus are in the center of a relationship, every problem can be solved.

Question: How do teenagers really feel about discipline?

TAMMY: Even though kids gripe about their parents' getting after them about something they have done, they really like it. The ones who don't get disciplined may brag about it, but down deep inside they really wish their parents would discipline them. My friends who don't have parents who discipline them are begging for it.

TIMMY: I agree with Tammy that the average kid really wants to be disciplined. The ones who don't ever get disciplined are not very enjoyable to be around. Nobody likes a spoiled brat! When Mom or Dad do discipline the child, it should be done in love and not in anger.

Question: What is the most precious part of your relationship to your family?

TAMMY: The family's relationship with God. I believe that if this is right then everything else that is needed will be ours. We feel that our relationship with God is not only personal, but through our whole family, we are related to him.

TIMMY: Time alone with just the family. We love other people, but we enjoy each other best of all. Things are not what most young people want; they just want to be with each other and be loved and needed.

Question: What makes young people rebel?

TAMMY: Too much of a lot of things. Some have too much of material things and have found that it does not satisfy. Some have too much free time and not enough responsibility. Some have too much of the wrong kind of discipline . . . not enough love and too much anger. Young people are angry when they do not find the answers to life at home. Their rebellion is a search for life.

TIMMY: Lack of love and attention. If parents are gone, or try to buy their children's love, or do not give them attention, there is trouble. I guess the main reason is that the devil gets into them and causes rebellion.

Question: What about the generation gap?

TAMMY: I don't know about it, because there is not one in my family or at least you don't notice it. There is a gap between the ages, but Jesus is the bridge.

TIMMY: Talk about the generation gap seems to me to be a form of rebellion. I think this is on the parents' part as well as the children. Some parents try to use the generation gap for an excuse to keep from becoming involved in their children's lives. I think that there should be sort of a generation gap and that the parents should have full control of the family. The father should be the head over the mother and the rest of the house. That is the kind of generation gap we have at our house.

Money management is not so much a technique as it is an attitude. And when we talk about attitudes, we are dealing with emotions. Thus, money-management is basically self-management or control of one's emotions. Unless one learns to control himself, he is no more likely to control his money than he is to discipline his own habits, his time, or his temper. Undisciplined money usually spells undisciplined persons.

ROBERT J. HASTINGS

The bride, bent with age, leaned over her cane,
Her steps uncertain need guiding,
While down the church aisle,
    with a wan toothless smile
The groom in a wheel-chair came gliding,
And who is this elderly couple thus wed?
You'll find when you've closely explored it,
That this is that rare, conservative pair . . .
Who waited TIL THEY COULD AFFORD IT!

UNKNOWN

7 Victory in Family Finances

It has been observed that problems relating to money are the most difficult problems in the marriage relationship. It is estimated that a minimum of one marriage in every five is in serious trouble because of money problems. Louis Evans in his book, *Your Marriage, Duel or Duet,* has a chapter entitled "Finance . . . A Fury or a Fellowship." In that chapter is this paragraph involving the problem of money in marriage: "There it is . . . the bombing of bills, and the fury of finance. The monetary maelstrom can wreck a home if we are not careful. Peace will only come with a well-thought-out program of finance. Over many a broken home could be hung this sign: UNTIL DEBT DO US PART."

This is a chapter about victory. There are families who are clearly in *defeat* over their finances. Yours may be one of those. If that is true, I want to tell you here with all the certainty at my command that better days are ahead for you if you will read and heed this chapter. There are other families that are merely *surviving* in the area of finances. There is worry and there are burdens, but they will make it if nobody rocks the boat. Then there are a few families who have found the keys to financial victory. We must not stop short of victory!

Financial victory is a necessity in the victorious walk with Christ. The adversary does not work on your strong points as much as he does your weak ones. You may be strong in prayer and biblical

75

exposition, but weak in finances. The devil will camp on that weak area and use that as a strike base for other areas. May I, thus, issue a challenge at the outset of this vital chapter? *Will you right now determine that you will not stop short of total victory in this important area of your life?*

We are going to discuss three important areas as we approach the finances of the family and the victory that God intends. We will observe the problems which impede victory, principles which invite victory, and projects which implement victory.

Problems Which Impede Victory

It would take a whole book to list all the problems in the area of family finances. We shall enlarge on just a few of the more common ones.

The love of money.—The Bible warns that the love of money is the root of all evil (1 Tim. 6:10). The first time I heard that I wanted to protest it, but when I turned to try to find one evil that was completely detached from the love of money, I could not find it. That same verse in 1 Timothy goes on to affirm, "Which while some coveted after, they have erred from the faith, and pierced themselves through with many sorrows." It was Ananias and Sapphira who met their death because of the love of money. Their tragic story is recorded in Acts 5. Judas had such a love for money that he was willing to sell his Master for less than $50.00! The bishop of the New Testament church was to be a man who was "not greedy of filthy lucre" (1 Tim. 3:3).

What is one to do when he realizes that this is his problem? The answer is simple. "Thou shalt love the Lord thy God with all thy heart, and with all thy soul, and with all thy mind, and with all thy strength" (Mark 12:30). If you will choose to do just this in response to the command of Jesus, there will be no room for love of money. We are commanded in 1 John 2:15 not to love the world or the things in the world.

Take God's side against the love of money in you. Renounce it and forsake it! The love of money will keep victory from your family life.

Misunderstanding the purpose of money.—There is in our world a gross misconception of the reason for the existence of money. Money is simply a medium of exchange. It has no intrinsic value in itself. Misunderstanding its purpose will lead to obsessions to get it and a mania for keeping it. The preacher in Ecclesiastes observed a "sore evil under the sun . . . namely riches kept by the owners to their hurt" (Eccl. 5:13). Failing to properly understand the purpose of money will also lead to abuses with the power that it seems to bring. Money in the hands of weak men is used for leverage in every kind of situation. Money in the hands of parents who don't understand is used to compensate for the lack of nurture that is really owed the children.

This problem has cost the man who has little as well as the man who has much. Only by seeking first the kingdom of God and his righteousness can a right understanding of money prepare the way for victory.

The catastrope of credit buying.—While credit buying has enabled many families to have things they never would have gotten otherwise, there is serious question in my mind of its right to exist at all, except in cases of rare nature. Until recently I was on what is called a "revolving charge account" for more than a dozen years. If I had the money that I spent on the interest on that account, I would have a mini-fortune. Young couples have unneeded pressures applied on their marriages by numerous pay-by-the-month plans which seem so innocent and non-demanding when viewed in isolation. By the time, however, that a young couple has a dozen such accounts or so of like nature, the situation is impossible. Would you like to get your family off the credit merry-go-round? I can tell you that I believe beyond a shadow of a doubt that this is the will of God for you. You can be sure of the support of heaven when you set your face to put your finances on a pay-as-you-go basis. I will have some suggestions with regard to this later on.

Keeping up with the Joneses.—We are bombarded with ads which show folks in supreme happiness possessing things which enhance their comfort. We are encouraged to covet the things that others have. Our children are brought into the picture through advertisement techniques. They simply must have the latest toy, the new innovation, the popular game, or the most up-to-date fashions. We must keep up regardless of the cost and this most certainly leads to living beyond our means. There may be some superficial satisfaction in keeping up with the Joneses, but the expenses up where the mythical Joneses live are prohibitive. The Christian family must make a choice between the Joneses in the neighborhood and the Jesus of Nazareth.

Greed in giving.—If there is one problem in finances which is more costly than any other, it is this one. It can never be proven on paper, but without varying the greedy giver is one whose spirit is starved. If Christ is to preside over your finances, there must be an end to greed. Greed is opposed to the very framework of God's universal plan. Giving is built into the very cycle of nature. All that God has made has joined in the great giving program. The design of greed is:

> Get all you can,
> Can all you get,
> Sit on the lid,
> And poison the rest!

Greed is never satisfied with getting. If you would get, give! It may be painful to convert a greedy giver to a cheerful one, but it will be the best business deal you ever made.

Robbing God.—The Bible makes it crystal clear that we are stewards of that which God has given. It is all his. We are to give at least one tenth of what we earn as a symbol of the fact that we recognize it all to be his. After this, our giving program begins. In the days of Malachi God declared that his people were robbing him in tithes and offerings. He then challenged them to trust him and prove him to see if he would not open the windows of heaven and pour them out such a blessing that they should not be able to receive (Mal. 3:8–10). Folks are still robbing God today. The family where there is a conspiracy to commit fraud against God cannot expect to walk in financial victory.

These are just a few of the problems which impede victory in the finances of a family. If you are caught in one of these, then look with me to the next area of truth.

Principles Which Invite Victory

I am going to share with you now the principles which helped liberate my family financially. I want to tell you that this reading may be detrimental to your present financial habits. I have related to you that the greatest miracle of our lives has been that which occurred in our home as husband and wife. The second greatest miracle has occurred in the area of finances. We had watched as all our plans for financial victory went awry. Nothing seemed to work! As hard as we tried we seemed to get deeper into debt. When God began to reveal to my mind some simple principles, I began to see why nothing had worked. These principles are simple, obvious, and biblical. Any plan of economy built on these principles will be sound. I want you to view with me what I will call "The Seven Principles in the Platform of Financial Victory."

Principle 1: God has all the wealth in this world and the next
  "The earth is the Lord's and the fulness thereof; the world and they that dwell therein" (Ps. 24:1).
  "Thine, O Lord, is the greatness and the power, and the glory, and the victory, and the majesty; for all that is in the heaven and in the earth is thine; and thine is the kingdom, O Lord, and thou art exalted as head above all. Both riches and honour come of thee, and thou reignest over all; and in thine hand is power and might; and in thine hand it is to make great, and to give strength unto all" (1 Chron. 29:11-12).
  God is not wanting for wealth. He has it all. Our first reaction is, "If he has it all, then why are his causes always wanting for money?" The answer is that though he has it all, his children have not learned how to appropriate it for his causes. God is the great resource from which come all things. His riches are unsearchable. His wealth is unlimited. This is the first principle in financial victory. He owns the whole thing and reigns over it all.
  If you cannot mentally comprehend this, just believe it by faith and proceed upon it.

Principle 2: God wants his wealth in circulation
  "For God so loved the world that he gave" (John 3:16). This precisely is God's disposition regarding all his wealth. He is ever

giving, giving, giving. He lavishes his wealth upon the world. He builds into the world a giving system filled with mutual beneficence. The earth is filled with gold, silver, precious stones, oil, and natural resources. The whole universe is a wealth of dazzling color. There are the clouds, the sun, the moon, the stars, the trees, and flowers. They are all giving! The rivers and fountains are ever flowing, giving!

Man has rebelled! He wants to get and keep. He has broken the cycle of the universe. He has robbed himself in robbing God for God's purpose was to give. God's desire was that man simply fit into the beneficial system of the universe and be its crowning creation.

Principle 3: All of God's wealth belongs to his children

With our membership in the family of God came the full inheritance of all that belongs to God. We are heirs of the covenant of promise (Gal. 3:29).

Jesus, in describing our inheritance, said, "He [the Holy Spirit] shall receive of mine, and shall show it unto you. All things that the Father hath are mine; therefore said I, that he shall take of mine and shall show it unto you" (John 16:14–15).

All of the wealth of God is within the family. It is ours! If you had great wealth would you be pleased to see your children living in poverty? Well, neither is God pleased to see you and me living as we do.

The great question remains, "How do we get that which is ours positionally to become ours practically?" The next principle answers that question.

Principle 4: The key to appropriation is giving

When God created Adam and Eve and fitted them into his program of eternal economy, there was perfect order. They were a part of God's great plan of mutual beneficence. There was a tree in the midst of the garden which was the Tree of Life representing the total resourcefulness of God. There was as much of everything as man would ever need within the context of obedience to the will of God. Man did not know what it was to suffer want. God's provision was complete. Man asserted his independence when he partook of the forbidden tree. He fell and as he fell, he moved into a new pattern . . . that of selfishness. Down through the centuries God revealed himself to man as a giving God, rewarding obedience and unselfishness. Men of God were men who had learned the secret of giving themselves.

Then God gave the world Jesus, the givingness of God personified. He was God's proof of this principle. God gave his Son and through his giving, received millions of children. God received through giving. Through Jesus Christ we can be saved, born again, regenerated. Through that new birth, we can be made over so as to be able to be godly again. Being godly, we can give as God has given.

Jesus sounded out this principle clearly when he said, "Give and it shall be given unto you; good measure, pressed down, and shaken together, and running over, shall men give unto your bosom. For with the same measure that ye mete withal it shall be measured to you again" (Luke 6:38).

If you family has a *getting* problem, in reality it has a *giving* problem. Giving is the key to getting! It all starts with giving. But getting is not the end. We give to get to give! The more we give, the more there is to give. God will see to that. If you are in a hole, start giving . . . now!

The principle which Jesus gives us so clearly in Luke 6:38 works in any area . . . not just the financial area. Give *love* and you will get more than you give. Give *joy* and you will get it back with interest. Give *concern* and you will be the object of concern. Give *time* and you will find more on your hands than you thought existed.

This principle is proved in a dramatic fashion in the final chapter of Job. There sat Job without enough of *anything*. He was short on friends, money, health, family, joy, love, and every other commodity which makes life enjoyable. Yet, the Bible says, "He prayed for his friends." At that very moment the Lord turned the captivity of Job! He had found the key! Give and it shall be given unto you. "And the Lord gave Job twice as much as he had before" (Job 42:10).

You may be sitting there short of everything. You may be thinking, "If I could have this or that I could get out of this." Friend, you are in a perfect position for faith. Start giving! You have nothing to give? Well, here is the answer to that . . . the next principle.

Principle 5: We are to give from his actual wealth instead of our apparent wealth

I want you to get this! God has plenty of everything. He has plenty of love, concern, compassion, time, money, power . . . you name it and he has plenty of it. All that he has is in Christ. If you are a believer, Christ is in you. That is your hope of glory (Col. 1:27). Therefore you have all that God has positionally. When we give, we are giving not out of what we have, but out of what he has. We can join David as he said, "For all things come of thee and of thine own have we given thee" (1 Chron. 29:14).

Our basic mistake in giving is that we are prone to give out of our apparent wealth. Therefore, we have the unexciting experience of giving only what we can afford. You ask, "Isn't that the sensible way to give?" Yes, it is, but it isn't the spiritual way to give. There is sense giving and there is Spirit giving. In the former you give according to your poverty. In the latter you give out of his boundless resources. There is a difference!

This is a mind-expanding concept and you will have to let it sink in until you start giving like your Father was rich. I will never forget when I began to learn this. We were in the process of raising a large amount of money. We challenged the people to find the mind of God in their giving and to give out of the wealth of God instead of giving what they could apparently afford. I began to seek to get the word from the Lord on the amount our family would give. The figure went out of sight! I was shocked, and I said, "Why I could not afford that under any circumstances." God seemed to reassure me by putting these words in my mind. "You can't afford it, but if I lead you to give it, I can afford to give it to you to be given." "If you can trust me to commit yourself for it, I can trust you enough to give it to you." There was no apparent manner by which this would be possible. And yet, at this date, the commitment has not only been fulfilled, but more than $1,000 has been given in addition. Not one payment was missed and the regular giving in the tithe and beyond was completely unaffected. *You cannot outgive God!* But it certainly is a thrill to try.

How do you give what you can't afford to give? Give out of his resources. They are opened to you through Jesus Christ. "My God shall supply all your needs according to his riches in glory by Christ Jesus" (Phil. 4:19). Whatever you choose to make your needs, he will supply. If you choose to make someone's illness your need, he has committed to supply that need. If you give yourself into a position of need, he has promised to supply it. We have just had too little need! We do not have God in our giving until we give so much that God has to come through to get us out!

You can literally give your way to financial liberty! If you would have more *wisdom,* start *teaching.* If you would have more *love,* start *loving.* If you would have more *money,* start *giving.* It really works! I have delivered this message in a morning service of a Bible Conference and have had folks come to the evening service beside themselves with joy. "It really works!" they exclaim.

But this is not all! There is more!

Principle 6: It is more blessed (profitable) to give than to receive

We do not know when or where Christ said it, but we do know that he did. "It is more blessed to give than to receive" (Acts 20:35). Until we really discover this, we will always say that with tongue in cheek. *Receiving* is the end to a selfish man. But *giving* is the end to the man who has found the secret. I am telling you the truth . . . just within the past few years have we found as a family that it is more blessed to give than to receive. And the more we give, the more we receive to give. We find that when we are prone to let up on the giving, the receiving lets up. It pays to do things God's way.

Peter had, perhaps proudly, exclaimed, "Lord, we have left all and followed thee." Jesus immediately replied, "Verily I say unto you, there is no man that hath left house or brethren, or sisters, or father, or mother, or wife, or children, or lands for my sake and the gospel's, but he shall receive an hundredfold now in this time, houses, and brethren, and sisters, and mothers, and children, and lands, with persecutions: and in the world to come eternal life" (Mark 10:29–30). How is that for an investment? A hundredfold!

And now the final principle.

Principle 7: God's power is released in hilarious giving

"But this I say, He that soweth sparingly shall also reap sparingly; and he which soweth bountifully shall reap also bountifully. Every man as he purposeth in his heart, so let him give; not grudgingly, or of necessity: for God loveth a cheerful [hilarious] giver, and God is able to make all grace abound toward you; that you, always have all sufficiency in all things, may abound unto every good work" (2 Cor. 9:6–8).

God is able! He is able all the time everywhere. But his glorious ability begins to be made manifest only when we begin to give hilariously, joyfully, spiritually!

Now I want you to review these seven principles as we list them together:

Principle 1: God has all the wealth in this world and the next

Principle 2: God wants his wealth in circulation

Principle 3: All of God's wealth belongs to his children

Principle 4: The key to appropriation is *giving*

Principle 5: We are to give from his *actual* wealth instead of our *apparent* wealth

Principle 6: It is more blessed to give than to receive

Principle 7: God's power is released in hilarious giving

You are free to check those principles against the Word of God and then to press them into service. You will discover that they make up a sturdy platform for victory in family finances.

Projects Which Implement Victory

I am not content with simple presenting principles. I want to promote some projects. May I challenge you and your family to these projects which I believe will transform truth into reality in blessings of all kinds?

Project 1

Check the foregoing principles against your life in actual practice. How many of them are being proved in your life right now? Reaffirm the ones that you have believed and applied. Affirm the ones that are not being proved in your life and ask God to thrust you into a life situation where that principle can be demonstrated. For instance, you flinched at the principle that says it is more blessed to give than to receive. You have not found that to be true. Ask God to put you in a situation where that principle comes to the front.

Project 2

Get your family together and survey your financial situation. Be frank and open about it. It should be a family affair. Find out the total of all your debts, especially your charge accounts. Approximate the amount of interest you are paying each month on all charge accounts. That is how much you could save immediately if you were on a cash basis. Do you desire to be on a cash basis? God desires it too! Begin to discuss some practical steps that could lead to a pay-as-you-go lifestyle. You will find the children getting into this project with delight. We can wear our shoes a few months longer. I can do with last winter's coat. The car will go at least another ten thousand miles before trade. We could eat out less. Set a goal for the D-DAY . . . Debtless Day! (This would probably not include such debts as your house.) Write that date down and take it to the Lord. Promise to cooperate with him to the limit of your ability.

My family did this less than two years ago. Getting out of debt was not foreseeable through natural eyes. We simply received the impression that this was God's will and claimed it. Within eight months it was done and more! I will not even attempt to tell you how on these pages. That would take another book. But it will suffice to say that I am not asking you to do something which I have not found to be proven in my family's experience.

Project 3

Get your giving records for the past twelve months at least. Does the total figure represent all that you would like to do? Is it representative of a tithe and more? Does the record indicate that you have a rich Father? You may not be ashamed of it, but are you delighted with it? Would the Internal Revenue Service agent be prone to look further into your situation if he saw your record? Is there a cause being pleaded right now and you don't know what you will give?

Decide with your family to ask God what he would have you give from the knowledge of his ability and not yours. Pray about it together and apart for several days. Come together and pool your impressions from the Lord. It will be much more than you would have considered giving before. Give it? It might scare you, but go ahead. Then watch God begin to prove the principles of prosperity!

Project 4

We have talked largely about money thus far. Now with your family turn to the needs of people all around you. Some need love, others need time and understanding, and still others need encouragement. You may feel that you need these too. Begin to give away what you feel you need the most. If it is time you need, then deliberately give time that you don't seem to have for someone else who is also pressed for time. Do the same with regard to love, encouragement, and happiness. Give and it shall be given unto you. Try it!

The lad with the lunch in John 6 gave his lunch for the Master's use. The disciples obeyed the Lord and received the particles of bread and fish. They gave and gave and gave some more. All the multitude was fed. The lad got all he could hold. They gathered up the fragments which remained and each of the disciples had a basketful left over. It will always work out that way. God has plenty in his storehouse and that plenty is yours as you obey him.

Lord, may the readers of this chapter experience the wonderful victory of Christ in family finances. Thus liberated, make their home . . . "one home under God."

If everything else in religion were by some accident blotted out, my soul would go back to those days of reality. For sixty years, my father kept up the business of family prayer. No hurry for business or market, no arrival of friends or guests, no trouble or sorrow, no joy or excitement ever prevented us from kneeling 'round the family altar, while our high priest offered himself and his children to God.

JOHN G. PATON

8 The Family Altar

> The greatest thing we as individuals can do for our-
> selves and our country will be to keep our families
> together in peace and happiness. There is no better
> way of doing our part for the homelife in America
> than by establishing the daily practice of family
> prayer in our homes; because families that pray
> together stay together.—*J. Edgar Hoover*

The Altar . . . a Historical Background

What is an altar? Why have an altar? What constitutes an altar?
Let us look at the background in the Old Testament.

Man needed no altar in the garden. All of life was an altar. The
whole garden was his cathedral. God walked with him in unbroken
fellowship. Then man sinned and judgment came. An altar was necessary for man to come before Holy God with a sacrifice indicating faith
and worship. Cain and Abel brought their offerings to an altar. The
difference in the offerings was not in designations of content, but in
disposition and intent. Abel's offering was accepted, but Cain's was
rejected.

The first act of Noah after God judged the earth through the flood
was to build an altar and make a sacrifice. The smell of the sacrifice

was to God a sweet savour and he said, "I will not again curse the ground for man's sake; neither will I again smite every living thing as I have done" (Gen. 8:21).

When the Lord appeared to Abram and promised him the land, Abram built an altar there (Gen. 12:7).

Abraham, under orders from God, took his son to the top of the mountain, built an altar and offered his son to God as God had commanded. He passed the test and God blessed him with a sacrificial ram to be placed on the altar. Isaac did not die, but Abraham died to Isaac in order to be alive to God. They called that place, "The Lord provides" [Jehovah] (Gen. 22:14).

In Genesis 26:24–25 God again promises blessing and greatness and they built an altar there and digged wells. You can settle down around an altar. God is there. Dig your wells and find water for your thirst!

In Genesis 28 Jacob, on the run, had a dream of heaven opened and God's messengers ascending and descending on a ladder. After the experience, he built an altar and called the place Bethel (God's house). He, however, tried to bargain with God. An altar is supposed to symbolize our willingness to meet God on his terms. Not until the great wrestling match in Genesis 32 did God subdue the proud and tricky Jacob and bless him after brokenness. Jacob established another altar and called the place Peniel [The face of God] (Gen. 32:30).

After Joshua won a resounding victory over the Amalekites in the Valley of Rephidim, he established an altar and called the place "Jehovah is our banner" [Jehovah-Nissi] (Ex. 17:15).

In Exodus 20:24 God gives instructions to build an altar and promises, "In the places where I record my name, I will come unto thee and I will bless thee."

When Moses was summoned to the top of the mountain to meet the Lord, he built an altar and sacrificed and interceded for the people (Ex. 24:4).

When Azariah preached under the anointing of God to Asa reminding him that "for a long season Israel hath been without the true God, and without a teaching priest, and without law" the king repented. He "took courage, and put away the abominable idols out of all the land of Judah . . . and renewed the altar of the Lord, that as before the porch of the Lord" (2 Chron. 15:3,8).

When Elijah was on Mount Carmel challenging Ahab and the prophets of Baal, he "repaired the altar of the Lord that was broken down" and called upon the God of heaven to answer. God answered and won the victory! (1 Kings 18:30 ff.).

In the memorable worship scene of Isaiah 6, after the confession of Isaiah, the angel took a live coal off the altar and touched his lips and there was cleansing (Isa. 6:6–7).

The altar in the holy of holies was the place where business was done with the God of heaven in behalf of the people and stood for the eternal sacrifice that would be made by which man's sins would be put away forever.

The altar is frequently mentioned in Revelation. It is the place where man meets God. It is the place to point men toward and from which men walk to conquest.

It is a place of intercession, confession, petition, and praise. It is a place where joy is received, burdens are left and lifted, and eternal business is transacted. It is a place of deliverance and dedication, happiness, and holiness.

It is a place from which issues the sweet-smelling savour of man's commitment into the nostrils of God.

It is a place where God and man are reunited and man and man are reconciled.

An old English bishop had the habit of beginning his day by saying before he got out of bed, "Lord, this bed is the altar; my body is the sacrifice; I happily and heartily yield it up to you!"

In the light of this historical background is there a lovelier name to be mentioned than that place where God meets man . . . an ALTAR? "I will praise the name of God with a song, and will magnify him with thanksgiving. This shall also please the Lord better than an ox or bullock that hath horns and hoofs" (Ps. 69:30–31).

Add to that lovely name the blessed title "Family" . . . and you have "Family Altar" . . . a storehouse filled with blessings!

The spiritual battleground around the home is well worn with skirmishes over the issue of the family altar. We have discussed it much, started it often, and watched it fail repeatedly. While our hearts advocate it as strongly as anything we know about, we seem alike incapable of making a success of it. Everything that has happened in our generation, it seems, has worked against the establishment of the family altar. Conditions of our day are definitely not in favor of the family altar. The family altar has fallen victim to a number of enemies. From home work to house cleaning and from television to PTA meetings, the nonfriends of family altar are myriad. It has fallen under the heavy blows of preoccupied papas, overworked mamas, and in-a-hurry children. Though it is extolled in books, magazines, periodicals, and sermons hundreds of times each month, we have to admit it . . . regular worship in the family . . . is seldom found. This is sad, but true!

You could bear the above facts out by your own testimony. You have begun your family altar so many times that it is embarrassing. You have tried everything and yet few who read these lines would be delighted to expose their family altar as ideal. Our family has not been immuned from these struggles. I do not hold up what we are doing as ideal, but we have learned some things that have been of tremendous help to our family altar. I am delighted to share some of these with you.

The family altar is a way of life. For years I wondered why it was so difficult, often embarrassing, to call the family together for family worship. I discovered that if you have to step out of context or change moods to come before God, you have a problem that must be solved. The fact was that there were some conditions which did not please the Lord about our home and family relationships. When we came before the Lord, with these existing conditions, we had to step out of normal context to speak with him. The tension, however slight, was always felt. The atmosphere at the altar is delicate. If God has not fitted in with your family schedule, it is not likely that a few moments at worship with the family will change the situation much.

Prayer that is preceded and followed by unkind words, displays of discourtesy, common unthoughtfulness, and continuing personal feuds is not apt to change anything, much less the world. We found that God needed to do a mighty work in us before we were ready for a triumphant family altar. Are you ready as a family to establish a family altar? Are there feelings, jealousies, resentments, deficiencies in courtesy, and manifestations of impatience which need to be cleared? Do you really want to worship with each other? We discovered that the motive of the family altar is vital. How many times did we start a family altar out of a sense of guilt and a desire to be a "respectable Christian family!" A family altar that will stand must begin with a desire to worship God with each other as family members. It will not become what it should be until it becomes a way of life. The context and environment of the altar will either nourish it or murder it. When the altar as an institution becomes as "in place" as the television, then the family can worship!

The family altar is a place and a piece of furniture. Not much emphasis is placed upon the family altar as a visible item. Our experience as a family has made us believers in the fact that this is of primary importance! Not until recently did we have a piece of furniture that could be referred to as a family altar. You can *sleep* without a *bed*, *eat* without a *table*, and *sit* without a *chair*, but the activities desired can be carried on with much less difficulty if you have furniture for it. You can also pray without an altar, but there is something about having a piece of furniture reserved for that activity that makes it easier.

If there is a piece of furniture, it will require a place out of the traffic pattern of the home. A special room is in order, but a special place in the living room is even better. Or, if the Lord has built your house, you may be sure that if you will just look, there is an ideal place for your altar!

We have just at this writing moved into our "Praise-the-Lord home." What was built as a small dining area just to the right of the entrance has become our place of prayer. Our altar is a platform four feet square and four inches high with a pillar in the middle for arm rests eighteen inches square and eighteen inches high. The kneeling platform is padded and carpeted. Although there is room for more, it is perfect for our family of four. When we kneel, we are facing each other.

As a place and a piece of furniture, it is a witness for all who enter our home. It seems to beckon us as we welcome and dismiss company. It seems quite natural that instead of walking by it, we should kneel at it. Just as the meal table is a visible invitation to eat, the bed a visible invitation to rest, the living room group an invitation to sit and fellowship, the altar is a visible invitation call to worship the Lord in the beauty of holiness and the happiness of family fellowship.

The family altar is a time and an event. If the altar is nothing more than a piece of furniture, then it is perfectly useless. In fact it is not an altar, because an altar is a place where we meet God! Our being there is what makes it an altar. There should be a set time when the family gathers at the altar for prayer. Preferably it should be at the beginning of the day. We have found the best time for this event is right before we leave for the day. The children are ready for school. I am ready for the day's work to begin. Mother is about to turn to her responsibilities after bidding the children good-bye. Right in the midst of our going, we stop. Each of us prays briefly, praising the Lord and reckoning the day as his, remembering any request of special importance.

This is not to say that we do not use the altar at other times. Our company often joins us there. When there is a misunderstanding or a crisis, the altar seems to be the place to go. I often go there alone after the family has gone to bed. We may stop at the altar on the way to a trip.

I am convinced that as long as my children live, they will never forget the family altar as an event which shaped their lives.

The family altar is an institution. This simply means that although it is a way of life, a place and a piece of furniture, a time and an event, it is even more , , , it is a concept. It does not depend upon so many square feet or a place to kneel. A family altar is an intangible institution which is as real when I am a thousand miles away as when I am at home. It is a thought pattern, a set of memories, a table of spiritual values. It is an institution that is real . . . as real as love, joy, peace, and anticipation. It is an institution that grows . . . as the building materials of concern, worship, praise, and discipline are added to it.

Because it is an institution of this type, we need never be without a family altar. Even when I am away (and I am away a great deal) we have family altar together. It is my habit to call home wherever I am (whenever possible) at 7:30 in the morning. The family knows that I will call and they are ready. They each get on a phone and we have our family altar. Expensive? Not when you think of the dividends. My wife's testimony is that ever since we began doing this, the sense of God's presence, the attitude of the children, and the atmosphere of peace are among the immediate results. I would recommend it to any traveling man as a must for his curriculum.

The family altar is a necessity for the family's spiritual well being. In the administration of the family life there must be planned everything that is needed for the physical, mental, emotional, and spiritual health. The prayer of Paul for the folks at Thessalonica was, "And the very God of peace sanctify you wholly. And I pray God your whole spirit, soul, and body be preserved blameless unto the coming of our Lord Jesus Christ" (1 Thess. 5:23). Notice the order in which Paul puts the care of the total person. The *spirit* is first, the *soul* is second and the *body* is third. That is the proper order in sequence of importance. The home that stands on solid spiritual ground will have the emphases in the same order. Many a husband would not think of neglecting his family's physical needs and yet will never lead them in a family altar or teach them from the Word of God. We have observed the exhortation of Paul in Ephesians 6:4 for fathers not to provoke their children to wrath. That warning is followed by these words, "But bring them up in the nurture and admonition of the Lord." What would provoke a child to wrath more than to awaken too late to discover that his parents had spiritually defrauded him by failing with nurture and admonition in the Lord?

Father, take the lead! It is your responsibility under God to establish and maintain the family altar. You are the president and professor of this institution. It will live and thrive on your initiative. Judgment will call for an accounting of your responsibilities as the head of the most important institution in America . . . *the home.*

The great Dr. W. B. Riley said, "The longer I live I am more persuaded that the average husband is making a mistake at the very point where he has supposed himself to be the most successful. He can delve sixteen hours a day and coin a mint of money, and construct a beautiful house and hedge it about by a great and attractive lawn, and multiply his automobiles, and increase the number of servants, and every bit of it will be accepted by the woman who is his mate as her natural right. And then he has no time left to be gentle, and tender, and gracious, and complimentary as in old days of wooing and poverty. Thus she and the children are almost certain to conclude that the affections are gone!"

That may be listed with Dun and Bradstreet, but on God's list he is a failure. Dad, what have you provided for the spiritual well-being of your family. What have you provided for your family that rust or thieves cannot touch?

The Bible speaks of a "shaking" in the last days in Hebrews 12. God vows once more to shake the earth until everything is shaken that is shakable. Then only those things which cannot be shaken remain. Listen to this: "And this word, yet once more, signifying the removing of the things that are shaken, as of things that are made, that those things that cannot be shaken may remain" (Heb. 12:27). What is that which cannot be shaken? The next verse says, "Wherefore we, receiving a kingdom which cannot be moved, let us have grace whereby we may serve God acceptably with reverence and godly fear" (Heb. 12:28). My friend, the only thing that cannot be moved is the kingdom on the inside of us. What is done in the home that is not of the kingdom of God is sure to pass. Only his kingdom is eternal!

Father, I call you to remember that your vocation is vital and your accountability is certain. "If any provide not for his own, and especially those of his own household, he hath denied the faith, and is worse than an infidel" (1 Tim. 5:8).

But what if the father, because he is lost, or because he is a carnal Christian, will not establish a family altar? Then mother, under God's delicate and dynamic leadership should seek her husband's permission to do it herself. Invite him to participate. If he will not, go ahead. The effect upon him will surely be immediate. Mother, if your children were being neglected physically, you would do whatever you had to do to see that food was on the table. If there was no shelter over their heads, you would seek to provide it. If there is no spiritual teaching and influence then see that it is provided by graciously seeking to establish a family altar through your husband's permission.

Steps and Suggestions for Establishing and Maintaining a Family Altar

Step One: Be convicted of the absolute necessity of the family altar. This is not an option if you are to be in the will of God as a family. The home under God will have such.

Step Two: Get the family together for a discussion of the vitality of and the necessity of a family altar. Ask each family member to pray about having it, when to have it, and under what circumstances. The

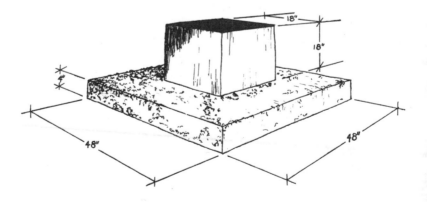

father (or mother, if he will not) should direct the suggestions and discussion. You might ask them to study the meaning of the altar in the Bible and prepare a brief report to be presented the next family meeting.

Step Three: Agree on the time and place for the family altar. You may desire to have the Bible study and the prayer time at different times and places. We have discovered that the breakfast table is a great time (either before or after) for the Bible study. The prayer time may be after everybody is ready to leave for the day.

Step Four: Begin the family altar. It will not maintain itself. Whoever takes the responsibility for it must maintain it under God. It will not be easy!

Step Five: You may wish to build that piece of furniture to be used as the altar. I have a detail of it drawn for you for that very purpose. You may want to prepare a special room or a place in an existing room in which to place the altar.

Step Six: Maintain your family altar in a planned fashion. Suggestions for doing this:

1. Make it brief. Do not draw this out over a long period of time. You can kill a family altar period by dragging it to death.

2. Make it biblical. The Bible can be interesting. I am going to suggest some projects with the Bible at the end of this chapter.

3. Involve the whole family. We learn by doing more than by listening.

4. Do not preach or chide when the children seem less than excited at first.

5. Stay open to suggestions by all family members for the improvement of the worship time.

6. Be serious, but do not forbid informality. Teach the children that to worship God one does not have to be "up tight."

7. Keep it interesting. Avoid routines. Do the novel and innovative things.

Ways to Use the Bible

There is no end to interesting ways to employ the Bible in family worship. It is a fantastic Book and we have tragically allowed the enemy to tame it down in our minds until we miss its glory. Here are some ways we have to enjoy the Bible.

Simple Bible Quiz   This is simply the asking of Bible questions to "contestants" which may include the whole family with the exception of the one who asks the questions. The one who questions may be a different one each learning period. Score is kept and friendly competition encourages more Bible knowledge.

Bible Password   The game is well known. Play it just like on television, but use biblical words.

Twenty Questions   The one who is selected to lead writes down a person, place, or thing that is biblical. The remaining family members then take turns asking questions until they guess the answer.

Who Am I?   The leader gives hints as to what he has in mind. For instance, he may select the ark of the covenant. The first clue may be, "I symbolized the presence of Holy God in the midst of His people." If the answer is not given, the next clue may be, "When someone tried to touch me in an unauthorized manner, he was instantly killed." If still no correct answer, the clues should get easier. "I contained a pot of manna." This is a thrilling game to children of all ages and adults as well. Keeping a score on each of these games makes it more interesting. Devise your own method of scorekeeping and rewards.

Bible Baseball   The pitcher is the questioner. Each family member may be a team. The "batter" calls for a one base pitch, a two base pitch, a three base pitch or a home run. He gets three "outs" or three misses or wrong answers. It works just like baseball and you can work out the details quickly. The three-base pitch, for instance, may be a question with a threefold answer. "Who were the three Hebrews in the fiery furnace?" If the batter answered it correctly, he would have a three base hit. He then might ask for a one base question and when that was answered, the "man on third" would be batted in! I suppose you could work out a Bible football game, though I have never tried it.

Bible Riddles For instance, explain this one: There was a man who lived to be the oldest man who ever lived, yet he died before his father died. *Answer:* Methuselah lived to be 969 years old and yet he died before his father because his father was Enoch who never died. He was translated without seeing death.

Another example: I once preached a sermon on the subject, "Three Bugs and a Rabbit." Where in the Scripture could the text be taken? *Answer:* (Proverbs 30:25–28. Three bugs are ants, locusts, and spiders. The rabbit (or rock badger) is the coney.

Children will surprise you with their ability to think up puzzles and other innovations for Bible learning.

Pop Quiz After a brief teaching period, call for a pop quiz. Grade the quiz and give all the right answers. This is more popular during the summer months as there are enough such quizzes during the school term!

Bible Crossword Puzzles These should be simple and have a time limit that is brief.

These are just a few. The possibilities are limitless. Work on them. Your family may put together a book of these for families across the world to use in their Bible learning period.

For the Prayer Time

Allow a moment for personal requests.

Give time for reports on answered prayer.

Talk about the different kinds of prayer (for example, praise, confession, petition). Give a specific instance or example of each.

Each family member should be allowed to pray briefly. Encourage variety in prayer. Discourage vain repetitions.

Keep a prayer list for the family as well as personally. This will greatly aid you in praying and will afford a wonderful source of inspiration in the multitude of answered prayers.

Be bold at the throne of grace. Ask for specific things so you can give specific praises.

Learn Scriptures by memory that contain prayer promises.

At intervals give time for each family member to quote a prayer-promise Scripture.

Encourage prayer all the time, not just at the prayer altar time. Crises of all kinds, needs, disappointments, tragedies, misunderstandings, and failures are all calls to family prayer.

Allow God to teach your children to believe that he can heal as well as provide in other areas.

Remember, "The prayer of the upright is his delight. . . . He heareth the prayer of the righteous" (Prov. 15:8, 29).

"Do you take . . . ?" These are the first three words of the question which precedes the repeating of the wedding vows in most marriage ceremonies. I am convinced that many do not tell the truth when they answer in the affirmative. To answer and affirm, "I do now take you . . ." is to acknowledge the receipt with pleasure of the husband or wife. God joins us together on this basis. "What God hath joined together, let not man put asunder" (Matt. 19:6). What happens after that will either show the participant to be a person of his or her word or a liar.

J. R. T.

Receive Your Family!

> Then the Lord God caused the man to fall into a deep
> sleep, and took one of his ribs and closed up the
> place from which he had removed it, and made the
> rib into a woman, and brought her to the man. "This
> is it!" Adam exclaimed. "She is part of my own bone
> and flesh! Her name is 'woman' because she was
> taken out of a man" (Gen. 2:21–23, TLB).

There is contained in this chapter an exercise that can change your life. It is a principle that reaches not only into the family, but into every area of life. The effect of the principle exercised will be immediate. With reference to family life, it is simply put in the title of this chapter, "Receive Your Family."

The Choice . . . Receive or Reject

Life is made up of choices. What one becomes is a result of his choices of what to receive and what to reject. The word adjures us to "hate what is wrong and stand on the side of the good" (Rom. 12:9). If one *receives* what he ought to *receive* and *rejects* what he ought to *reject,* he *becomes* what he ought to *be.* He receives Jesus and rejects the devil. He chooses God's will and rejects his own. What he receives influences him and gives him the full benefit of its character . . . whether good or bad.

Formally receiving what we believe brings us to salvation and continuing to put your faith into action in actual receiving will continue to bring the benefits of our salvation. Receiving is like withdrawing from the account. We know that what we need is there, but it does not become ours in actual experience until we receive it.

What we do not receive, we reject whether we intend to or not. We may not at all feel a sense of rejection, but that is what it amounts to. A blessing not received is a blessing rejected. Fail to claim it and it will fail to come.

Do You Take This _____?

Most wedding ceremonies have within them the taking of the formal vows. These vows involve a formal reception on the part of each for the other. Generally the minister asks, "Do you take this man to be your lawful and wedded husband?" The question is repeated to the husband regarding the wife. The reply is, "I do." In many cases the vows are repeated. "I _____, take you _____, to be my lawful and wedded _____." In the ceremony the basis of the whole matter is their commitment to receive each other as they submit to each other. On the basis of such a mutual commitment and mutual reception they are pronounced husband and wife. They have given themselves to each other and they have received each other. (Or at least they say!)

Adam Received Eve

Adam had probably heard God say that it was not good that he be left alone. God further said, "I will make a helper suited to his needs" (Gen. 2:18, TLB). God then began to form out of the ground every beast and fowl and brought them to Adam to name. I am sure that Adam's mind was on his business, but I cannot help but think that in the back of his mind he was looking for that promised "helper." He named all the creatures that God brought to him and the Bible says, "And whatever he called them that was their name. But still there was found no proper helper for the man" (Gen. 2:20, TLB).

Then God does the unexpected. (Doesn't he generally?) He caused a deep sleep to come over Adam and while he was asleep God performed surgery and took out one of Adam's ribs. From that rib he fashioned the first woman according to Adam's needs and his own desires. He then presented her to man. Man's response was enthusiastic. He would give her a name as he did all the other creatures, but more than this he would *receive* her.

Let me paraphrase the *reception proclamation* Adam made: "This is what I have been looking for! She is a part of me, flesh and bone. This is precisely why a man leaves home and stays with his wife. The two become one!" (Gen. 2:23–24; my own paraphrase). I see at least four things revealed in this *acclamation of acceptance:*

I see, first, an *acknowledgement of reception.* God brought her to Adam, but now Adam acknowledged the receipt. He was saying, Lord, this is it; this is exactly what I have been expecting! It is perfect! I could not improve on it at all. *This is now* bone of my bone and flesh of my flesh."

Second, I see an *expression of possession.* "This is bone of *my* bone and flesh of *my* flesh." He is not only delighted with the character of what he sees, but he formally commits himself to be responsible for her. She is not only his possession, but his responsibility. She will call him from other charges to care for her. He needs her and needs to be needed by her.

Third, I witness a *commitment to togetherness.* He will *leave* in order to *cleave.* The word "cleave" literally means "to adhere" or to "stick to." The doxology of Adam in receiving Eve not only was an approval of what he saw, but a commitment to leave all else and spend his days with her. They would be one! It was not to be an intermittent fellowship, but a total adherence.

I see, fourth, a *proclamation of purpose.* Though this is an implication, it is a solid one. There is purpose pervading all that Adam says in this decisive declaration. He has received this "woman." He has claimed ownership and responsibility. He has committed himself to a life of togetherness with her. He stands, now completed, to fulfill the purposes of God.

Just as Adam received Eve, we need to receive each other. We may already "belong" to each other in a technical relationship, but there is not the mutual benefit that should accrue from such a union. The act of receiving will transfer it from a theoretical *truth* into a *tremendous treasure.*

Every family is now experiencing *reception* or *rejection. Reception* brings release. *Rejection* brings resistance.

Husband, Receive Your Wife

Receive her as being from God. It was no freak accident that you got together though it may have appeared to be as far as you are concerned. God allowed it to happen! Thus you can rightly say that she is a gift from God. Listen to this verse: "Every good gift and every perfect gift is from above, and cometh down from the Father of lights, with whom is no variableness nor shadow of turning" (Jas. 1:17).

Husband, I know that she is yours in every sense of the word, but have you *received* her? Have you simply formally acknowledged that she is God's gift to you? Have you simply declared that everything about her is designed to work out the plan of God for your sanctification and perfection?

How have you responded to her seeming flaws and faults? Have you rejected her to a measure because of these? You indeed have done one or the other. If you are resentful over a fault she seems to have, you have rejected her at that point. You have said, "I will not tolerate this in her! What you should have sought is the reason for that particular condition. You should have asked, "What is God trying to teach me through this trait in my wife?" Thank God for her apparent imperfections, because they are qualities that God has designed to minister to your apparent imperfections. Simply because your wife is different from you does not mean that she is full of faults. You may be serious and somber; she, flighty and frivolous. You may be disciplined and organized; she, disoriented and disorganized. If you complain about her "opposites" you are rejecting and not receiving. As long as you reject her, God cannot do what he desires to do in you through traits that are in her. When you receive her, he can then use her traits to bring you into balance together. No longer are your *opposites* apparent. What is apparent is your *balance.* He has used her to place everything into perfect balance.

Have you ever wondered why God put together so many "opposites"? He has a habit of putting the quiet and matter-of-fact with the loud and boisterous; the perfectionest with the reckless; the quick-tempered with the easy-going; the overbearing with the meek; the retiring with the aggressive! It is because God is not near so interested in a situation without pressure and conflict as he is in getting us conformed to the image of his Son. Thus, God is pleased to work through each of us in the life of the other toward perfection. Like two rivers meeting, different in force, content, and flow, but merging their qualities into an everdeepening and ever-widening channel of power, the husband and wife, with differences as vast as those rivers are joined together into a powerful whole.

There she is . . . God's gift to you. Receive her, not as you see her, but as God sees her . . . just exactly what you need to be perfected. She is to you what Eve was to Adam . . . a helper suited to the need. Look at her from God's viewpoint and receive her.

A Husband's Proclamation of Reception

Father, in Jesus' name, I now receive my wife. I accept her as she is as a gift from you. I receive the fact that every quality in her is aimed at perfecting a quality in me. Being a gift from you, she is perfect, holy and without blame before you in love. I love her because I love you. I declare that love to be absolutely unconditional. No quality in her will deter or discourage that love. She is bone of my bone and flesh of my flesh. She is what I need to be complete. Thank you, Father, that in your perfect wisdom you have given her to me. I happily and heartily receive her. Forgive me for rejecting her at any point and causing conflict through complaining. I cannot reject her in any manner for to do so would be to reject a part of me and thus, to reject you. I will continue in this disposition regardless of what happens. In Jesus' name, Amen!

You may have been married one, ten, or fifty years, but now inform her that you are here and now *receiving* her as a gift from God and giving thanks!

Wife, Receive Your Husband

Rejection is a common cause of broken homes. The sad thing about it is that most of it is far from deliberate. It is unconscious and unintentional. Many a husband has felt rejected when in reality he wasn't. Many a wife has responded to felt rejection by returning rejection. Rejection breeds rejection. Wife, your husband has been given to you for protection and provision, as well as productivity. He has been given to you for your fulfillment. The things in him that arouse your anger and impatience are there to be used of God to work out some condition in you to the pleasure of God. Reject them and you have robbed yourself. Receive them and God's intended benefit will come.

Receive him as your authority. Receive him in every capacity mentioned in chapter four; receive him as *provider, protector, priest, prophet, professor, partner,* and *pal.* Declare before God and the world that he is to you both a *lover* and a friend (Song of Solomon 5:16).

Through him is the privilege of producing life in the likeness of God. You cannot do it without him. If you are complaining about him or to him at any point, you are in part rejecting him. Ask God's forgiveness and your husband's and receive him.

A Wife's Proclamation of Reception

Father, in Jesus' name, I now receive my husband. He is God's gift to me. Forgive me for putting more emphasis on what he *isn't* than on what he *is.* I receive him as my lord, my life, my keeper, my head. He is what I need to be productive and purposeful. I give thanks over problems and potentials affirming that these exist to be used of God to work out his plan in me. I have taken his name in the stead of mine. I now receive him. I celebrate that reception with praise and thanksgiving. In Jesus' name, Amen!

Now inform your husband that you are receiving him. Ask his forgiveness for manifested rejection. "Do you now take this man to be your lawful and wedded husband?" You can now say "I do" with new zeal.

Parents, Receive Your Children

Familiarity, too often, breeds contempt. The holy relationship between parents and children often degrades into a cold war between noncommunicating factions. Gratitude is buried under the debris of thoughtlessness and unforgiven offenses. Rejection reigns. We may hold it to be tolerance, but in reality, it is passive rejection.

Parents should be continually assessing their wealth. Their offspring are the nation's greatest natural resources. They are their treasures. With the birth of each child comes the resounding declaration from heaven, "I have not lost total confidence in humanity!" Your children were brought into being through divinely ordained means. It was natural and legitimate. They are yours only as he allows it.

Have you been busy harassing them with this, "Why-when-I-was-your-age business"? Have you been so busy rejecting their hair, their clothes, their music, and their culture that you have finally rejected them? While you continue respectably providing for their physical needs, are you denying them the things they need most . . . acceptance of them as persons?

I sympathize with your dilemma in being willing to accept the philosophies and practices of all who are young today. But someone must receive them as they are in order to release them to become what they ought to be. Your rejection will only breed more rejection in them.

As man in general is God's means of reflecting his image and reproducing his likeness, your children are the means of extending your life and likeness. Reject them and you have rejected yourself. Receive them and you have received yourself as God's purposeful instrument.

Have you ever lost a child? Have your arms ever ached to hold what wasn't there? For nine wonderful, anticipation-filled months we waited for our firstborn. It was during seminary days on a Friday in July that he came. With reckless abandonment, I used the phone to call the world as if I owned the company. I was the father of a boy! But less than seventy-two hours later I watched him die. I knew all the things to be said to the bereaved and we said them to ourselves.

The comfort of the Holy Spirit was ours. We thanked the Lord as did Job . . . "The Lord gives and the Lord takes away, blessed be the Name of the Lord" (Job 1:21). You can imagine our joy as we received our second born exactly two years from the very hour as the death of our firstborn. I have often thought as I have remembered those days of loss of how easy it is to take for granted those gifts of God to us. How many folks have watched their children die emotionally, love-starved and attentionless, victims of a "too-busy" syndrome?

I find joy in receiving my children in prayer as gifts from God. As I do it almost daily I find that it enhances my appreciation of them and my fellowship with them. Matters of temporal importance become trivial before the eternal investment afforded of time with *my* children. As I take God's view of my children, I see them being formed into his image and receive it as a finished matter. I have seen the end from the middle and the matter is settled.

A great man lay dying. None of his children were at that time serving the Lord. As he died, he said thanks over each child, receiving them in the Lord. He was asked how he could give thanks for them as they were. He remarked that he was giving thanks for what God had promised him they *would* be. Not too long after his death every child was in the service of the Lord devotedly serving him!

Parents' Proclamation of Reception

Father, in Jesus' name, we receive our children. They are gifts from heaven to us. Forgive us for impatience with their immaturity. We receive them to give them back to you to be used to complete and perfect us that we in turn might be used to perfect them. They are what we need as parents. We receive them not as our eyes behold them, but as you intend to make them . . . perfect. We are delighted with your gifts to us and ask forgiveness for being less than completely pleased with them. They are to us a delight and a pleasure. We could not have made them more perfect than you have made them. We are happy to receive them here and now! In Jesus' name, Amen!

As you have shared this concept of *receiving* the family with the children, inform them of your unconditional love and acceptance. This will move them into position of receiving you.

Children, Receive Your Parents

Children, your parents will never cease to be a great resource of limitless wealth. Through early days, they will nurture and care for you. Through teen-age years they will weep and laugh with you, play and pray with you, and continue to be the one stable rock upon which you can stand. And when you have left home and they return to life with just each other, they will be to you your prime supporters, their past kindnesses affording pegs upon which to hang a happy set of memories. And you will return to home ever now and then and relive hours long since gone and go away stronger because you have been there. When you are older and they have gone, their influence will escort you through every day of life blessing you, stabilizing you, encouraging you, and challenging you to be to yours what they have been to you.

You can receive them whether they are forty, eighty, or gone! Then all the wealth afforded from parents to children will begin to be yours experientially.

Children's Proclamation of Reception of Parents

Father, in Jesus' name, I receive my parents as gifts from you. They are to me your provision of direction and dynamic. They are my authorities, but also my counsellors. They are my judges, but also my defenders. They are my walls that separate me from evil, but my doors through which I walk to the good life. I receive them as perfected in your mind from eternity to eternity. I praise you for my parents! In Jesus' name, Amen!

Children, Receive Your Brothers and Sisters

Not everyone is blessed with brothers and sisters. God blessed me with two of each! I was the youngest boy with one sister older and one sister younger. For more than twenty-five years we have been in our different worlds only to visit at enjoyable intervals. How pleasure-filled are the memories of my boyhood with that crowd that was my family! We lived life to the hilt! We played hard, fought hard, and worked hard. At this writing I am enjoying in my spirit *receiving* my brothers and sisters. The words are more precious to me now than they have ever been. I have *brothers* and *sisters.* We don't often see each other or correspond or even converse by phone, but we are still brothers and sisters.

The daily ritual of receiving each other will prevent those selfish offenses against each other that betray our love. Enjoy your brothers and sisters by receiving them.

Children's Proclamation of Reception for Each Other

Father, in Jesus' name, I receive my brothers and sisters. They are to me resources of joy. I happily invest my life in them. I love them not only for what they are, but for what you are making of them. I thank you that we will spend eternity together and that eternity has already begun. I receive them now in Jesus' name, Amen!

If you are living with them let them know of this response. If you are separated from them write or call to review your commitment to receive them.

Receive Your Family

One by one you have received them . . wife, husband, children, parents, brothers, and sisters. NOW RECEIVE THE WHOLE FAMILY! Let memories flow, get reckless in your appreciation. Lavish thanksgiving on your family . . . all of them. Receive them as from the Lord!

Father, right now I receive my family. At this moment the most beautiful words in the world are . . . home, family, dad, mom, wife, husband, son, daughter. My family is the means you have given me for heavenly living in pre-heaven days. In them are all my anticipations met, all my needs supplied, and my need to be needed fulfilled. You are using them to complete me. I thank you that I am a part of this family. I receive them all. In Jesus' name, Amen.

He has given us the family. Now, UNDER GOD, let us receive

them! You may wish to lay aside the book at this point and write every family member a letter of reception. Whether you mail the letters, personally present them, or hold them in your own files for years, you will discover a great blessing in doing it. The book will be waiting for your return and you will be more ready for the reading of the rest!

In the Meanwhile (a Postscript)

I am moved by a number of dramatic events and a time of great stirring from the Lord to share with you more relating to this vital principle of receiving each other in the Lord.

After the major part of this chapter had been written, I was confronted by a counselling situation with a husband and wife who were deadlocked in anger and resentment. Though it is not best to go into details here, I can share with you that they knew as well as I the marriage could not go on under the prevailing circumstances. They not only knew it, but frankly admitted it.

I listened to them for a few moments. Much of the resentment had by this time subsided and we could communicate in a cordial fashion. He was frank and honest in sharing his feelings. He was more intelligent than his wife and could not understand why anybody could not be as smart as he was. The same was true with his children. She responded to this by saying that she was exactly what he made of her. She naturally responded to the opposite as he would launch a tirade against her. If he complained about the housework being less than efficient, she would do less housework and eat more and gain more weight. If he griped about the money, she would become more resentful about the whole money situation. They were in a rejection-resistance deadlock!

As I listened to them my mind went back to the material the Lord had given on the chapter you are reading. I turned to the husband and said, "You lied at the marriage altar!" He looked surprised. I continued, "When you were married, you signed a certificate and said that you were taking this woman to be your lawful and wedded wife. You were lying. You did not receive her and you have never received her. By refusing to receive her you have made her more like what you don't like. You have locked her into being what you don't like by refusing to receive her." I shared with him the concept of receiving your mate as a gift from God. Taking God's point of view and seeing her as perfect and as a means of perfecting him, he could then witness her release to begin to become what he had always wanted her to be. The fact was that what he wanted her to be, he was forbidding her to be by rejecting instead of receiving her.

God turned the lights on inside that man's mind! He said, "You're exactly right! I have never received her. I have rejected her and tried to make her over." It became obvious that he had done the same with the children. He was seeking to make them what they ought to be without the Lord. At times he got so frustrated that he became violent. This is the result of disenchantment which is due to the fact that no report of faith has been received from the Lord. When that man decided to look at his wife as a gift from God and at the report that God had already called her to be holy and without blame before God, he fairly rose out of his seat. "Where have I been all my life?" he exclaimed. "Why hasn't somebody told me this before?" he asked. Well, you can imagine the results from there. Of course, the wife was not without fault, because she was as busy reacting as he was acting and rejecting. She was as busy rejecting as he was.

I simply asked both of them if they were ready to receive each other as from the Lord and praise him that they were in God's eyes destined for perfection and designed to make each other perfect. Their reply was in the affirmative. We knelt at the altar in our home which was only a few feet away and they took each other as husband and wife! Their testimony days later is that nothing in all their married lives has so affected their marriage and home atmosphere.

Further Revelations

As I saw this happen in the lives of this couple, I began to further investigate the dynamic of this principle. My thoughts went back to the time when we were forced to bring my wife's mother into our home. While I gave consent, I did it without really receiving her in my spirit. There was trouble with a capital "T"! We fussed and fought and fumed. What has happened since this is simply fantastic! I have witnessed a total personality change in my mother-in-law. My wife began to receive her mother and so did I. Reception commands reception and brings release.

As I began to consider other realms where this principle might be effective, I discovered that it is as broad as life. Jesus said in Matthew 18:5, "And whosoever *receiveth* one such little child, receiveth me." He further stated, "And whoso shall offend one of these little ones which believe in me, it were better for him that a millstone be hanged about his neck, and that he were drowned in the depths of the sea." The difference in the destiny of people is made by receiving or rejecting.

There is transforming power in receiving love. Love gives, but love also receives. When we love someone with Christ's love, we receive them. We who have been received and accepted in the beloved can then release that love through us and receive others. This is evangelism and this is ministry. What is outreach but the act of *reaching* out, *receiving* the lost in Jesus' name, and *releasing* them to life in Jesus?

And that is the order of the Christ-life; reaching out, receiving, and releasing!

If you would be living proof of this principle, let me request of you that you check closely your own heart to see if there is someone whom you are rejecting. This does not have to be hate, resentment, or bitterness. It may just be passive disregard. Choose something or someone and begin to receive . . . that is, to thank God for that person or thing, and accept. If it is a thing or circumstance, you will see that situation begin to make a difference in you as God designed. If it is a person, you will begin to behold the work of God in that person and in you through that person.

This will work on a total stranger. You may have some time on a plane trip, a wait in line, or in your office at work. Deliberately reach out, receiving that person as God's gift to you to love and bless. As you respond with love and blessing, you will witness a release in that person.

Happy receiving . . . in your home, in your business, in your church, and in your world! Remember that Jesus reminds us that when we receive others, we receive him!

I have counselled many married couples. Though I have not carefully checked it, I fear that the losses may outnumber the wins. The marriage was not saved. Because the preacher is the last resort, often minds are already made up. The damage has already been done. In all those I have counselled who have come on the verge of divorce, I have yet to find one in which the breakup began over big things. Generally there were a few little matters over which there was little communication and finally total estrangement. The expense of neglect in little things is great indeed.

J. R. T.

The secret of a happy marriage is simple: Just keep on being as polite to one another as you are to your best friends.

ROBERT QUILLEN

10 Watch the Little Foxes

Take us the foxes, the little foxes, that spoil the vines (Song of Sol. 2:15).

The enemies may be small, but the mischief done is great. A little spray of blossom, so tiny as it can scarcely be perceived, is easily spoiled, but thereby the fruitfulness of the whole branch may be forever destroyed. And how numerous the little foxes arel Little compromises with the world, disobedience to the still, small voice in little things, little indulgences to the flesh to the neglect of duty, little strokes of policy, doing evil in little things that good may come, and the beauty and the fruitfulness of the vine are sacrificed.—*J. Hudson Taylor*

In the Song of Solomon is a strange statement. The scholars have not agreed as to its implications. It is thought by some to be a reference to an ancient fertility rite. But as it sounds in all the versions I have read, it strongly suggests the point of this chapter . . . namely that little things often are the spoil of the great. It is generally the minute, the microscopic that begins the work of destruction of a marriage. Large things may later come to administer the *coup de grace,* but the little things long neglected were the culprits.

For this reason, this chapter is a warning to all married couples and members of the whole family to *watch the little foxes!* We are going to look at three areas which involve the little foxes: the *distraction* of the little foxes, the *detection* of the little foxes, and the *destruction* of the little foxes.

The Distraction of the Little Foxes

Have you ever wondered why the term "little foxes" was used? The answer may be a key to preventing many problems in marriage. A little thing has an advantage in most cases. It is not expected to be of much consequence and thus often overlooked. Little things within the marriage relationship may seem so trivial that they would never be suspicioned as carrying weight enough to knock the marriage out of commission. The fox is such a wily little fellow that his name is synonymous with trickery and cunning. We speak of a "sneaky" person as "foxy." The *little* foxes are the most cunning of all. Their cuteness often decoys and distracts.

Our society has so drawn attention to various conditions in marriage and family relationships that everyone expects it as the normal. Television exalts relationships as quite "average American" where everybody yells at everybody else and "knock downs and drag outs" are everyday occurences. It is cute and humorous over the television screen, but it is terribly painful in real life. The *little foxes* that work to destroy the home are often tolerated because they are source material for many a punch line in a sick joke. An unfortunate game many Americans play is that of *sick satire* over problems we had rather laugh at than face and solve.

I am now speaking to you about your home. "Watch the little foxes!" There may be working right under your nose those little conditions which are not unlike those in other normal homes, but what is unpretentious now may be unmanageable later. If you will be determined to take care of the little foxes now, there will probably be no reason to fear the large lions later! Are you willing to read this chapter with an open mind and look for those little things that have the capacity of wrecking a home? I believe that you will find if there is an immediate reckoning with reality now regarding the little foxes at work in your home, there may not have to be that sad reckoning with regret later on.

The Detection of the Little Foxes

There is the little fox of *discourtesy.* Courtesy is a vital part of marriage and the family. The first five letters of the word spell "court." The lack of common courtesy has been a part of a pattern that has caused the deterioration of the *courtship* of a marriage and eventually to bring it to the *courtroom* for termination. Who can know the sturdiness of a marriage continuously reinforced by displays of kindness and courtesy? The taking of the hand for a moment on the street, the opening of the door on the car, the pausing to allow others to go first . . . may seem trivial, but are tremendous in building the integrity of a happy home.

It is sad, but true that if most of us were as discourteous with our friends and co-workers as we were with the members of our families we would be both friendless and jobless.

Recently, on some property we own in Colorado, we watched several great pine trees die. It wasn't lightning or an intruder's axe that did it. It didn't take an earthquake or a forest fire. A little beetle did it. He was no larger than the tip of a ball point pen. He simply bored through the bark, circled the trunk of the tree, and cut off the life supply. The trees were just as dead as if severed by a mighty storm.

A little beetle or a pesky fox may be all it takes to do the job. Watch for tell-tale signs of fading courtesies in your home. Make a determined effort to reestablish old-fashioned family courtesy. Deliberately design patterns of courtesy. It will be fun as well as helpful.

There is the little fox of *unthoughtfulness.* Those simple little displays of thoughtfulness during the days of courtship drove pegs upon which to hang a happy set of memories. What happened to that innovative mind that was forever giving birth to ingenious tricks of thoughtfulness? Where is the phone call on a pressured day? Where is the special note left in the right place, saying just the right thing? Where is the momento that says volumes without words and awakens pleasant memories? Are they not in place any longer? It may seem like a poor epitaph over the grave of a wrecked marriage, but it may be true . . . "I just never thought!"

There is the little of *unthankfulness.* Thoughtlessness leads to thanklessness. A little energy here yields great effect.

"Thanks, Mom, for a wonderful meal!"

"Thanks, Son, for carrying out the trash."

"Thanks, Daughter, for helping Mom in the kitchen."

"Thanks, Dad, for taking us to the game!"

"Thanks, Family, for just being His and mine!"

Thankfulness is a plant that grows under the sunshine of spoken words. It develops best in the soil of watchfulness.

There is the little fox of *preoccupation.* Life is busy. No one can deny. It is busy for Dad, Mom, son and daughter. We develop our uniquely individual schedules early these days. Dad leaves early for work. Mom rushes the children to school. There is shopping, extra board meetings, out-of-town trips, cheer-leader practice, football workout, and a myriad of other things, ad infinitum. A real-estate agent tried to sell a modern young girl a home. Her reply to this attempt was,

"A home? Why do I need a home?

I was born in a hospital, educated in a college, courted in an automobile, and married in a church;

I live out of the delicatessen and paper bags;

I spend my mornings on the golf course, my afternoon at the bridge table, and my evenings at the movies;

When I die I am going to be buried at the undertaker's.

ALL I NEED IS A GARAGE!"

It may be true that we cannot solve the busy-ness problem, but we do not have to succumb to total preoccupation. There is a little fox we could do without!

There is the little fox of *nagging.* Though this is generally designated as a favorite indoor sport of women, it certainly is not confined to the fairer sex. Papa can nag with alarming persistency. And sometimes the children develop the art very young, especially when there are two good advanced teachers around teaching them how! God manifested his distaste for murmuring when he told Moses in Numbers 14:28, "Say unto them as truly as I live, saith the Lord, as ye have spoken in mine ears, so will I do to you." Nagging is a steam shovel that carves out its own pit of environment.

There is the little fox of *criticism.* Nothing eats away at the foundation of a marriage like criticism. It takes its worst destructive form in public. The husband or wife is obliged to point out flaws in the mate in the presence of others. This is discouraging, depressing, disgusting, and destructive. Two words will suffice here . . . *stop it!* Deliberately take note, set a guard at your lips, and stop it!

There is the little fox of *poor appearance.* Appearance was of prime importance during the days of courtship. Anything of prime rating during the days of courtship should not be forgotten in the days of the family. I do not know that there is such a word, but sloppy ways make for it . . . *misappearance.* In my thinking *misappearance* is worse than *disappearance.* Your appearance was important at the wedding. It is still important in the dining room, the living room, the den, and the bedroom. Take nothing for granted. May I seek to make such an appearance that everyone would think I was campaigning for re-election as the father and husband of this family.

Wife, what did you look like when you greeted your husband when he came in from work today? Are you interested in having some good constructive fun? Let me make this suggestion: Tomorrow doll yourself up for your husband's homecoming. Put on some of that perfume he brought back from his trip too long ago. Cook a supper fit for a king. Get out the candles. Turn on the music. Get the smelling salts ready! He may faint! But when he comes to, you will have a delightful evening. Appearance is important and *memorable.*

The little fox of *too much television.* The T.M.T. Syndrome is a plague among us (Too Much Television). I recently made the public statement that the devil could control anyone's thought pattern to a great degree who watches television more than one hour per day. I am convinced that time alone will tell how greatly television was used by the enemy to waste prayer time, deter Bible study, and undermine the moral and spiritual values of our generation. I am not advocating doing away with the television. (Which might not be such a bad idea!) What would be of great help is a critical analysis of your family's television viewing habits, a strict screening of programs that were "on limits," and a study of the format, intent, and innuendo of certain programs selected.

You might even try the "Baltimore Experiment" with your television at intervals. In this experiment a group of Christians decided to seek to find out what conditions would prevail in "televisionless times." So they unplugged their television sets and turned them around, screen to the wall! The bare back part of the television set was a mute reminder visible to all. The results were most interesting:

Family members would come in, walk over to the television, and by force of habit reach for the "on" button.

They would then sit down somewhat embarrassed and attempt to make conversation in an awkward manner with whomever was in the room.

They then would begin to get interested in each other and carried on a more sensible conversation.

They began to get acquainted with these "strangers" with whom they lived and rather enjoyed their company.

They began to develop such strange practices as simple conversation about life and each other, helping with the homework, and engaging in Bible quizzes.

By the way, I don't remember if I heard the end of the experiment. Do you think it possible that they got so involved with each other they couldn't find the time to turn the television back around?

Watch the little fox of T.M.T. (TOO MUCH TELEVISION).

There is the little fox of *money madness*. It is not always the inordinate love of money that makes it a problem for the modern family. Many are caught on the treadmill of financial expediency and cannot seem to find a way to get off. The madness goes on. It is possible to move from *getting money to live* to *living to get money* without even knowing it! The wife is forced to work. Soon what was begun as a temporary arrangement becomes a permanent necessity and the wife faces working for the rest of her life. It is true of many that they are so busy making money to pay for what they have purchased that there is no time left to enjoy it! This fox is sometimes not so little and appears to be more like a roaring lion.

There is the little fox of *mobility*. Ours is a mobile society. In a recent year the phone company in our city registered moves in 45 percent of the homes where there was a telephone installation. In a well-known denomination recently over 33 percent of the official board moved during the year. It does not have to be so, but it is possible that a family can develop a "mobile syndrome." This renders community interest nil, prevents deep spiritual involvement and works against fostering meaningful friendships. "We can always move," may become the family's cop-out as area problems are faced and feared. In the move the problems that were known were exchanged for problems that are unknown. Only superficial and deceptive appearances indicate that the move was a wise one. Finally, these as have hundreds of others, give way to disillusionment and disappointment. The little fox strikes again!

There are many other "little foxes." By now you should have become "fox-minded." Look for them, search them out, prepare to trap them.

Destruction of the Little Foxes

Praise the Lord that there are no seasons to protect these little foxes. Not even the SPCA (Society for the Prevention of Cruelty to Animals) would protest the destruction of these "little foxes." Allow some suggestion for dealing with these enemies of happiness in marriage:

Learn their tracks until you can detect where they have been and when.

Identify the particular "brand" of fox and deliberate his termination.

Plan a campaign of courtesy.

Launch an offensive of thoughtfulness.

Land a whole division of gratitudes.

Declare war on preoccupation.

Call a moratorium on nagging and murmuring.

Make criticism that is not constructive "off limits."

Adopt a total program of neatness and attractiveness.

Demand equal time for God and family with the television OFF.

Transfer your bank account to HIM. Though you still sign the checks, He is giving approval.

Pray to stay! It just might be God's will that you stay put and take root.

Like a nation's defenses there must be guards stationed around the homes of America. I am a believer in angels. The Word tells us that the angels are "servants sent out in the service [of God for the assistance] of those who are to inherit salvation" (Heb. 1:14, *Amplified Bible*).

The home that is determined to be spiritual is a prime target for the "little foxes." Watch them!

When an ordinary citizen fails, a small circle of friends take notice and sympathize and mourn. When a preacher fails, an ever-widening circle of people form a multitude of mourners and scorners. When a regular family breaks up some cry and speak regretfully. When a preacher's family breaks up, the vibrations of that breakup reach every soul he has ever won, every couple he ever married, and every life he ever touched. For this reason the preacher's home is under satanic assault and there must be a constant guard lest this fortress fall.

SELECTED

11 The Preacher and His Family

> The adversary would rather spoil one preacher's home than a dozen of any other kind. In doing so he has touched hundreds of other homes. No home is under attack more than the preacher's home.—*Selected*

Don't close the book! Even if you are not part of the parsonage set you need to know what is in this chapter. Every Christian needs to understand something of the perspective from the view of the parsonage.

At this moment I am reminded of upwards of a dozen preacher friends whose homes have broken up or are now in trouble. As a direct result of these there will be at least a dozen more breakups. The fall out of this unholy explosion will be experienced as long as time exists.

Some of the greatest preachers in history had problems with their family.

Eli was a great priest and had a profound effect on Samuel's life. But he did not have time for his boys. Their lives were a reproach and a shame to Holy God. His sons, Hophni and Phinehas, desecrated the ministry of God, violated the purity of womanhood, and refused the faith of their father. Their simple biography is found in 1 Samuel 1:12, "Now the sons of Eli were sons of Belial; and they knew not the Lord." They broke the heart of their father and upon hearing the news of their death and the ark of God being taken by the enemy, Eli fell backward and broke his neck. The wife of Phinehas, at about the same time, died in childbirth. Before she died she named her child "Ichabod" which means "the glory hath departed."

David was a great man . . . a man after God's own heart. Yet he was a failure as far as his son, Absalom, was concerned. Absalom was rebellious and did everything he knew to get attention for himself. He built a monument to himself. Yet, in the midst of his rebellion he consented to be brought back to his father. David refused to see him for two whole years. Absalom made plea after plea for the privilege of seeing his father and plea after plea was refused. Finally, through the intercession of Joab, David consented to see Absalom. The king greeted his son with a kiss. This was all too late. Absalom's rebellious pattern was set. His death, in the midst of rebellion, was untimely and tragic. The wail of many a father is heard in the ever-growing chorus sung by David:

> "Oh, my son, Absalom, my son,
> My son Absalom,
> Would God I had died for thee,
> Oh, Absalom, my son, my son!"

2 Samuel 18:33

Surely these stories are recorded for our benefit upon whom the ends of the world are come! May we learn from their mistakes.

The Preacher and His Wife

The position and plight of the preacher's wife is a peculiar one indeed. It is one of the highest callings in the kingdom to be a preacher's wife. And yet, there are thousands of unhappy preacher's wives in the land today. They feel imprisoned in a glass house where their business is everybody's business. She is forced without recourse to share her husband with everybody in the land who desires his time. She must, it seems, please everybody in the parish while filling a myriad of roles all the way from dishwasher to taxi driver. And after all this is done she must please and satisfy her husband and assist him in serving the people.

The preacher will have great difficulty rising above his home. It will either limit or enlarge his ministry. We have already said that the preacher's home is his ministry. To fail there is to fail in one of the most vital areas to which he is called to minister.

This seems to be a difficult area with which to reckon for the minister. The preacher is pampered, praised, adored, admired, and exalted by many. The wife and family are apt to be overlooked unless care is exercised by the preacher to give them the attention they need and deserve. In most cases if other members of the church and their families were neglected as sadly as the pastor's family, there would be serious trouble.

Allow me to share a story which has, in part, already been shared. As my wife and I began our marriage, everything was toward "my ministry." We were sincere and believed that this was the right approach. It sounded good and noble. For seventeen years of our lives together we put "my ministry" first. What we really did was put me first. Under the guise of protecting and enhancing my ministry she poured her praise, her energy, and her vitality into "my ministry." Every now and then the resentment would pour out without either of us knowing why. As God began a new work in my life I began to see that I was sacrificing my wife on the altar of ministerial success. She drained her own life, pouring it into the ministry without proper return for her spiritual benefit. My wife was a person who had no pastor. I was busy caring for the needs of others and no time was left for her and the children. They got me at night after every duty had drained me of energy and compassion.

When I recognized by the grace of God that my family was the first facet of my ministry, I began to face my responsibility. My wife and I came to the position of commitment to each other's needs and accepted each other as gifts from God. I can tell you now, as I have stated before, what has happened in our home is the greatest miracle of the whole visitation of God that has come upon our lives.

I have found in my wife a great prayer partner, a trusted advisor, and a true friend. She had been none of these before to a great degree, because I would not allow her to be. Because of our ignorance, both hers and mine, we were so intense about *my* ministry that *her* ministry was totally neglected and undeveloped. When she *became* my ministry, her ministry began to develop. We began to pray that God would use her to share the message of victory through Christ in the home. God has graciously answered that prayer and the ministry is growing every day. Now, *our* ministry is beginning to evolve!

I would not want to deceive the reader into believing that our household has become a place where there is never a problem. I can tell you that as God trusts us with problems, our love for each other equips us to take an objective position and allow God to deliver us in it until in his wisdom he can deliver us from it.

The Preacher and His Children

"There goes the preacher's kid!" is generally said with some derision. The preacher's children are, in most cases, spoiled by the membership and expected to behave like miniature saints. In most cases they only have a dad, at best and never know what it is to have a pastor. The fellow they call "Dad" hardly has time to be that, much less their pastor.

No preacher intends to neglect his family and defraud his children of a proper upbringing. Yet the rate of spiritual casualties is appalling with children of preachers. The preacher cannot find in the nobility of his calling and vocation any proper justification for neglecting his children. The fact that he is doing the work of God does not change the matter appreciably as far as his children are concerned. In fact it may cause them to have less respect for a God who seems to take all their father's time and leaves none for them. Many a preacher father has placed his children in a position of having to compete with God for their father's attention and interest.

In the midst of a time of struggle regarding the conflict of family demands and the demands of the ministry, I read an article in a denominational periodical entitled, "God Never Called Nobody to Be Stupid." I have not forgotten the title, but I have forgotten some of the details of the story. As I remember, this was the essential thrust of it:

The author was a young man who was serving out a prison term for writing bad checks. He was blaming no one but himself, but he was making some observations that seemed to be in order for all preachers. He did not have the benefit of a father as he was growing up and thus, was robbed of one of a boy's greatest privileges. He got into trouble and there he was in jail. In the article he said that it didn't make any difference where his father was . . . the issue was that he was not where he was needed. One child's father may be in the corner bar and another's may be attending a committee or a convention. The first lad's father may spend his off hours in the bar and the latter's father has commitments every afternoon and evening. The state of the father may be different under God, but the state of the sons is the same . . . they both have missed the benefits of having a father when and where they needed him. This was a shock to me because I had been justifying myself in spending night after night doing work of the Lord. Surely, I thought, the Lord would make up for the time that I missed with my family. The lad stated further in his article that it did not make any difference to the children where their father was . . . they were still without a father. Nothing could be used to compensate or rationalize for his absence. He was not there! And whether he is chasing around in immorality, boozing it up at the corner bar, making a million-dollar business, or keeping the church program going . . . the issue is the same: The children were without a father.

I never forgot that article. It had a profound effect on me. I became convicted that like men I had often criticized, I was sacrificing my children on an altar of success. While our civilization has almost obliterated ancient practices of human sacrifice, we are practicing a wholesale legalized and respectable human sacrifice in our own sophisticated day. Whole families are being placed on the altar and sacrificed to the gods of success. Not all of these are unbelieving homes. It can happen and is happening in many a preacher's home.

Preacher, take time for your children. When God began to touch me at this point, I had a schedule that involved brief trips of two or three days that could not be changed. I was impressed that God would be delighted to provide funds for me to take one of the children with me on various occasions. As the Lord led, I would inform the authorities at school that my son or daughter was going with me on a trip. Until Jesus comes and beyond, neither Timmy nor Tammy will forget those hours together in Florida, Arizona, and Washington.

There are passages of Scripture whose context is in question, but whose implication seems to be important. I use one of those here: "They made me keeper of the vineyards; but mine own vineyard have I not kept" (Song of Sol. 1:6). This today is the sad cry of many who have been called to tend to the vineyards of the Lord. May it not be so with you.

Problems and Perils Peculiar to the Parsonage

It is hard to compete with God and the Church. A woman and her children would know more about how to combat another woman's affections for their father and husband. But what are they to say when he is called out for crisis counselling just as they are about to sit down to enjoy a meal for the first time in days? Shall they "demand equal time" with God? A wife can tell her businessman husband that she had rather have a little less money and a little more of him and be looked on as wise and noble. Let a preacher's wife demand a little less ministry and a little more of her husband, and she is counted as selfish and faithless.

No home is in as much danger of being over saturated with religion as the preacher's home. Many a preacher's child has gotten so "sick and tired of church" that there is a reaction that extends into adult years for them. Many churches demand that every member of the preacher's family be in every meeting that opens the church doors. With over saturation there is deadening familiarity with things divine. Familiarity often breeds contempt. Contempt gives place to the devil.

The preacher is often a target of criticism and opposition. The results of this may be manifold if not handled correctly. It may embitter the preacher and cause him to take out his resentment on the family. It may embitter the family and cause them to take it out on God. It can serve as an opportunity for the whole family to be schooled to be like Jesus. The psalmist affirms: "Thou hast enlarged me when I was in distress" (Ps. 4:1).

The parsonage is a glass house. What goes on inside is everybody's business. That is as it should be. The man who lives in it is their pastor, their guide, and their spiritual shepherd. Everything in his life is under observation and weighs heavily in the important matter of spiritual trust. He can never say of anything he does, "It is nobody's business!" His life is everybody's business. To fight against this is to develop an attitude of defensiveness that invites attack and leaves one more vulnerable to the devil than before. If your life as a preacher is transparent and pure, you will not mind your parsonage walls being made of glass. Purity and integrity invites inspection and investigation.

Loneliness is often a peculiar peril to the parsonage. It is not the loneliness of being alone. That is usually easily solved. It is the loneliness of being a stranger in a crowd. Often the problem of the preacher and his family is that they are acquainted with everybody and intimately involved with nobody. Some preachers even believe that intimate friendship with any member of the church is forbidden because of his office.

Fear is another peril which often stalks the parsonage in a manner peculiar to that vocation. A wrong step, an ill-timed statement, a bad public relations move can result in a terminated pastorate. Finances are cut off immediately. Other churches suspicion a "churchless pastor." Like Job, he may say, "That which I feared is come upon me!" Many a pastor's ministry has been wrecked by an untimely dismissal and his inability to react properly to it. "Heavy, heavy hangs over your head," is the caption of many a preacher's portrait. The demand is to develop a winning team or else!

Have I drawn a bleak picture? It is by design! These and many other problems and perils are to be found in preachers' homes across the country. I suppose that I have known all of them at one time or another. My statement of them, however, has not been intended to draw pity for the parsonage occupants. To the contrary, I want to share with you how you as a Christian can help make the situation pleasant to all and glorifying to God.

Neither have I intended to imply that the folks who have surrounded my ministry have been unfair or thoughtless. I have been privileged to serve this one congregation since I was twenty-four years of age. My wife and I came fresh from the seminary and a country pastorate. Our folks have loved us and nourished us, praying for us and growing with us. Both of our children have known no other church, but this.

Because our people have helped us so much, I can write the next paragraph from the vantage point of the position of pastor of a vital, thoughtful, and insightful congregation. I can suggest some things that you can do for your pastor to enrich his life in order that he may be used of God to greater enrichment of your life.

Liberate Him to Love and Serve

The position of pastor has become impossible in the minds of many. He is expected to heal without a degree in medicine, counsel without a degree in counselling, keep books without a degree in accounting, and administrate without qualifications for administrating. In the meantime he must visit the sick, the dying, the newborn, the troubled, and the disgruntled. He is expected, in addition to all this, to stand and preach like a Spurgeon or a Truett and smile with love when he hears someone say, "What a deal he has! A couple of sermons a week and he has it made!"

Liberate your pastor! He has been called to do a spiritual job. It will largely be confined to the ministry of the Word and prayer. Anything that anybody else can do should be done by someone else, because there are enough things to do that only the preacher can do to take his entire time. There are more able administrators in the church than the preacher, in most cases; there are those who are more adept accountants than he is; and those as keen in counselling procedures as he is.

The first deacons were appointed in the midst of a murmuring of a group of deserving folks who had been neglected in the daily ministrations. The purpose of their appointment and ordination was that the ministers may "give themselves to prayer and the ministry of the Word" (Acts 6:4).

When you liberate your pastor, you have released him to be what you need to minister to you. You will have liberated him to become to his family what they need and deserve. God will be pleased to pour out His blessings without limit upon such a situation.

Pay Your Preacher a Living Wage

As God loves a cheerful giver, he loves a church that cares for its own. The salary scale of preachers in America is atrociously low. Many men with the same educational qualifications in the church make four or five times as much as the preacher. It is true that he is not in it for the money, but that is no reason to penalize him with poverty! The preacher should make at least a median wage to the congregation in which he serves.

Remember that money is coined personality. How you give and live with your money generally reflects your spiritual standing and your whole personality. Let a church develop in getting by with paying its help as little as the law allows and it will pervade the whole personality of the church. To the contrary when the church "pulls out the stops" and decides to believe the Bible when it says that God is able to make all grace abound toward us that we being sufficient in all things may abound to every good work, the personality takes on confidence, trust, and excitement (2 Cor. 9:8).

In a measure, money is coined love. When the preacher looks at his paycheck, he is reminded of how much you love him. While he is not a money-worshiper, he knows when he is loved.

Be Understanding of His Family

His children may need to stay home from church every once in a while to get their homework as yours do. Don't begrudge his day off or their vacation trip. My congregation has taught me the meaning of love, care, and thoughtfulness. They have given myself and my family such love and understanding that we know beyond the shadow of a doubt that the greatest privilege in the world belongs to us, that of being their pastor. My children will never resent being "preacher's kids," because of our understanding congregation.

Be a Friend to the Pastor's Family

He is like you, a human being. He has feelings, fears, failures, anticipations, and pleasures just as you do. A word of thanks, helpful and constructive criticism, or deed of kindness can serve to the delight of all.

Love Your Pastor!

Enough said! Love is patient, kind, and envies no one. It is never conceited, rude, or selfish. It is not quick to take offense and keeps no score of wrongs. It delights in truth and there is nothing it cannot face. There is no limit to its faith, its endurance, and its hope (excerpts from 1 Cor. 13, *The New English Bible*).

Pastor . . . Help Yourself!

I have spoken in your behalf to your people. Launch an all-out offensive of love. Love your wife! Love your children! Love your larger spiritual family! Love them unconditionally; love them lavishly; love them recklessly; and love them consistently.

Feed the flock of God. Be instant in season and out. Open yourself to your family and people. Love isn't afraid of being hurt. Determine that your home will be a seminary where your family is taught the verities of eternity, a love-station where love-starved folks can find the scarce commodity.

Give and it shall be given to you, good measure, pressed down, shaken together, running over. Give time, give love, and give yourself. With the same measure that you give, it will be given to you.

Pray everyday with your wife and children. Be sensitive to their needs when there would be every human reason to be preoccupied with the problems of your ministry.

Be content with what you have where you are. God is not apt to take you anywhere else until you can learn to stay where you are happy with his will!

Your family will reflect all your personal reactions. If you are happy, they will be. If you are selfish and accusative, so will they be. If you are loving and understanding, they will be the same. If you are Christlike in times of pressure, they will also be.

Yours is the highest calling in the land. Never become so preoccupied as to spend one day unappreciative that God, in his grace, has called you to an office that the angels would leave heaven to occupy.

You are the head of your family. You are the shepherd of a flock of families. You are setting the example of what a spiritual head of the family should be. It will take all you have and his fulness to be what you ought to be.

May your home be truly . . . "one home under God!"

Jesus began his ministry of miracles at a wedding feast. He was invited there. His presence made the difference. He turned a desperate dilemma into a memorable miracle. He will make the difference in your home. Invite him in! Let him not abide as a guest. Allow him to be host. He will replenish diminishing supplies and preside over your home with full provision and power. Whenever and wherever he takes over, there is a miracle!

SELECTED

12 When Jesus Takes Over the Family

Jesus Christ wants to be Lord and Saviour of you as an individual. Then, he wants to be the Lord of your marriage. If he is, then the home you are building will abide in lasting peace and blessing. If he is not the spiritual head of your home, you will find that you will never experience all of the blessing that God has for you in marriage. Jesus said, "Without me ye can do nothing" (John 15:5).—*Tim LeHaye*

The first miracle was performed within the surroundings of a wedding feast. It was the first link in a great chain of irrefutable evidences of the deity of Christ and his power with God and men. This miracle is ideal for establishing what happens within the framework of those strange phenomena that extend natural law as we know it and impose the power of God upon human needs.

There was a wedding and now a feast. Jesus had been invited along with his disciples. His mother was there. It is very possible that it was a cousin or kinsman of Jesus who was getting married. This is at least hinted by the fact that Mary seems to have had some responsibility or intimate concern beyond that of an invited guest. The story is found in the first eleven verses of John 2. The presence of Jesus at the wedding feast denotes at least three things:

One, he was invited by someone in a position of responsibility.

Two, he accepted the invitation and thus this was an indication of approval.

Three, he was sociable and obviously enjoyed visiting with the other wedding guests.

The presence of Jesus was the most important fact of that gathering. Yet, until the crisis, his presence was relatively unknown and he visited with the guests in obscurity. His presence there is the reason for us knowing about the story. By the way, does anyone know the names of those who got married? The fact that Jesus was there outweighed every other factor in importance.

This miracle affords us a clear opportunity to see what happens when Jesus takes over.

Jesus as Guest and Host

At first Jesus was in attendance at the wedding feast as a guest. We see a change in capacities as he later became the host. Mary played a vital role in this transition. Knowing that he was more than just her son, she came to him in the midst of the problem and presented it to him as if he could do something about it. His reply was not a rebuke, but a reminder that there was a right time for doing what needed to be done. Then dear Mary said something that, if heeded by all, would save the world. She said, "Whatsoever he saith unto you, do it." Evidently Jesus did not wait long. He took over the situation and the result was, "This beginning of miracles did Jesus in Cana of Galilee" (John 2:11).

I call you to be reminded that "in him all things consist" (Col. 1:17). He is the answer to the scientific dilemma of the cohesion of the cosmos. In other words, he is the glue that holds this whole thing together. When he is in a situation, any situation, he is the power by which that situation moves into proper perspective. When he moves into position to impose the will of heaven in that set of circumstances, there will be memorable results. That may be in your home, your business, or your school. When he takes over, three things always result:

1. Jesus addresses himself to human need.

The need was presented. Mary informed her son that they had run out of wine. Surely this is representative of the fact that the world is full of things that diminish in their supply. Can you name anything in this life that you cannot run out of. We see folks all about us who have run out of things. Some have run out of hope, others have run out of joy, and still others have run out of love. The supply is diminished. There is shame, embarassment, and misery. Marriages have run out of fulfilling purposes. Churches have run out of expectant enthusiasm. Individuals have run out of any reason to live.

This is where Jesus begins! Jesus is for failures. Sin is failure. When a man realizes that he is a sinner, he realizes that he is a failure. Jesus stands ready to do His work, but He does not begin until there is an admitted need. Can you find a miracle that was performed where the platform was not a positive need or failure on the part of man. Let's investigate some of them.

He performed the miracle of the loaves and fishes in the midst of the failure of man to provide adequate food for the multitude. The need was the launching pad for his miracle.

He calmed the storm when the disciples had run out of confidence. There was need presented in their fear. He rebuked them as having little faith, but they did have enough to call upon him.

He touched the man who had the need of sight. He brought light into his world of night. He started with a need.

He calmed the tormented soul of the wild man of Gadara. There was great need and Jesus moved upon it to perform a glorious miracle.

He forgave a woman who had failed to keep herself pure. She had run out of purity. Yet, when she came to Jesus admitting a great need, he fully forgave her.

He spoke to a paralytic who had laid in the one place for thirty-eight years and had about run out of hope. He heeded the command of Jesus and took up his bed and walked. Jesus commenced with human failure and need.

He raised the widow's son who had run out of life.

He came into the world to address himself to the fact of human failure and need. "For the Son of Man is come to seek and to save that which was lost (Luke 19:10).

He is the positive supply to man's need. He is the answer to your family's dilemma. He is ready to provide what you have run out of. That is his business.

Don't be afraid of the fact of need. This is simply the appearance of Jesus inviting you to watch a miracle in progress. And the one great characteristic of that which Jesus gives is that *it does not run out.* The wine that Jesus gives does not numb the brain and sicken the soul. It gladdens the heart and lifts the soul. It secures the heart against fear and the supply is limitless. God has plenty of all that he has which is everything.

The failure of man is apparent. His life is full of fear, disease, hate, confusion, ignorance, depression, and discouragement. Have you run out of something. Have you failed? Jesus is for failures! If you have need in your family and in your life, he is ready to address himself to that need.

The key command at this point is: "Whatever he says to you, do it!" If you are ready to move at his command and obey him to the letter, He is ready to meet your need.

2. He invites human cooperation.

Jesus uses human instruments. Wherever one was available he made use of it in every miracle. In this one he used water pots and believing people. Any old pot that is available to him may be used in a miracle. These happened to be pots with a religious significance. They were used in the purification ceremonies of the Jews.

Jesus used what was on hand. He is not through with the family or the church today. Don't discount something because it is old. It may be just an old waterpot. But he can make use of it.

Those fellows on hand did what he commanded. He told them to fill the waterpots with water. They directly obeyed and filled them up to the brim. Without question or deliberation they simply did what he said. He further told them to take pitchers of whatever was in the pots to the governor of the feast. I wonder what went on in their minds during that whole process. Whatever it was, they still steadfastly obeyed. That is what is required for a miracle.

In your home life, the same is true. Jesus is ready to supply whatever you have run out of. He will use you in what he does. Somewhere within the context of their obedience the miracle took place. The water had turned to wine. Man had provided the water and obeyed the Master and he had done the rest.

3. He reverses human inclination.

When Jesus takes over, there is a third and most important thing he does. He reverses human inclination. Human inclination is to start with the best and then serve the inferior. The flow of humanity in this world is downward.

A thing is new for a while. Then it begins to age and deteriorate. The house, the car, the suit and everything else in this life is in a state of decay.

The process of death is at work in this world. It is the work of the devil. When sin set in, decay began. The nature of humanity is to enjoy the best first and then settle for what is left later.

The custom at the wedding feast was to serve the good wine first and when everybody had drunk a great deal, then the wine that was inferior. This is precisely the method of the devil. If the devil served his worst first, no one would follow his line. He cannot afford to show the eventuality of serving him to his would-be followers.

Listen to what the governor said when he had tasted the water that was made wine: "Every man at the beginning doth set forth good wine; and when men have well drunk, that which is worse: but thou hast kept the good wine until now" (John 2:10).

You have saved the best til now! What a statement! The governor of the wedding feast described in that statement the nature of the kingdom of God. You have saved the best til now! I cannot think of one commodity in this life that God did not give about which you can say that.

Amid all the polluted streams in this world going downward, ever downward, there is one going the other direction. It is getting better and better. Those moving in that stream can all say all the time, "You have saved the best til now!"

Is not this your testimony? Is not your salvation richer today that it ever has been. If you are walking in the Spirit, the answer is yes. As we walk in the Spirit, we are being conformed to the image of Christ. Everyday that the Spirit is allowed to work, we are nearer to the image of Christ. We may say of every day, "This is the best."

About thirty years ago, I met the living Christ and asked Him to enter my life and be my Saviour and my Lord. That was the greatest moment of my life . . . at least up to that moment. A little while later he called me to preach. It was still better. I could have said then, "You have saved the best til now!"

God has continued to work in my life. Every day with Jesus is sweeter than the day before. Everything over which he presides gets better and better.

When Jesus takes over a business and does it his way, it moves from glory to glory. When he takes over a church, the best day is today, and tomorrow is a better one. When he takes over a home, the best is always now. When he takes over an individual, the sweetest is saved until now.

Human inclination in marriage is quite apparent. There is a fervent display of love in the days of courtship. That comes to fulfillment in the early days of marriage. Then, according to human inclination, the vocal and visible signs of love begin to wane. They feel less and less. Whereas they felt before that they could eat one another, now they wish they had! Attrition sets in. Preoccupation holds sway. Even human love without Jesus decays. Humanity serves the best wine first.

But Jesus reverses human inclinations. A couple meets Jesus. Their love explodes and the fall out is felt all around. He touches their love with his and it grows and grows. Abundant life is a quantity and a quality which is plenteous in supply.

And it will go on and on. It will continue to get better and better. One of these days the trumpet will sound and we will be caught up with him in the clouds. On the way we will surely be able to shout, "He has saved the best til now!" We will reign with him on this earth for a thousand years until righteousness covers the earth as waters cover the sea. He will have saved the best until now! Cataclysmic events will climax this earthly scene. There will be a new heaven and a new earth. He will have saved the best til now!

Then a billion years from this day, we will still be rejoicing in the glories of our Lord and his Christ. He will reign forever and ever. Yes, a hundred billion years from today we can still say, "You have saved the best til now!"

This happens when Jesus takes over. He addresses himself to human need. He invites human cooperation, and he reverses human inclination.

He will do that in your home when he is allowed to take over.

I especially want you to note the closing statement in the narrative of that miracle. "This beginning of miracles did Jesus in Cana of Galilee, and he manifested forth his glory, and his disciples believed on him."

He manifested forth his glory. He revealed his potential. His disciples had never seen him work a miracle before. They had followed him, leaving all else behind. Now Jesus steps into a new dimension as far as they were concerned. They were as surprised and shocked as all the rest. When conditions are right Jesus will do that which divulges his real power. A miracle is the unveiling of the true nature of Jesus. They saw him in a new capacity. Have you allowed Jesus to begin his miraculous ministry in you? Have you witnessed the beginning of miracles in your life? The great question is not, "Have you begun your public ministry for him?" It is, "Has he begun his public ministry in you?" He began his ministry of miracles that day at the wedding feast. Let us see the ensuing result.

His disciples believed on him. Had they not believed on him before? Of course they had. But now he has enlarged the glory that was visible and they are now obliged to believe on him at another level. We are ever having to believe on Jesus. With every manifestation of his glory, we are drawn to believe on him at a deeper level.

As he begins his miraculous ministry in your home, you will be moved to deeper and more committed belief.

He has the right to reign in your family. Will you extend to him his right? The results of his take-over are essentially the same. He will address himself to your failure and need. He will use human instruments, and he will manifest his glory.

The result will be that many will believe on Him. One home under his rule will influence history more than all the armies that ever marched.

Jesus, take over our homes and make them each . . . "one home under God."

"They were all filled with the Holy Spirit." The words are wonderfully simple, and yet express a truth surpassing understanding. What a vital difference the coming of the Spirit in his fulness to their hearts made to those first disciples. The weak became strong; the timid, bold; the carnal, spiritual. . . . We may understand the verse to mean that the Holy Spirit took entire possession of them to the full, and imparted to them, to the fullest extent of their capacity, his grace and power.

THOMAS WALKER

The Spirit-filled life is a *farce* if it is not a *force* in the family, bringing it to its highest expression of God's order. If it doesn't work in the family, it isn't genuine.

SELECTED

13 The Family and the Fullness of the Spirit

> Use the present opportunity to the full, for these are evil days. So do not be fools, but try to understand what the will of the Lord is. Do not give way to drunkenness and the dissipation that goes with it, but let the Holy Spirit fill you" (Eph. 5:16–18, NEB).

What the Will of the Lord Is

The Bible teaches that God's will for the Christian is a life of continuing fullness and control of the Holy Spirit. There is only one alternative to the Spirit-filled life and that is a life of backsliding. Just as the Spirit-filled life is the will of God for the individual, it is the will of God for the family unit. *The Spirit-filled life is a family affair.* We spend more time in the contexts of family living than anywhere else. What happens to us as individuals will eventually shape the corporate structure of the family.

After the seven last words of Ephesians 5:17 which are, ". . . what the will of the Lord is," two commands are given, one negative, the other positive. "Be not drunk with wine . . ." (Eph. 5:18) is the negative command and holds a vital key to the understanding of what the fullness of the Holy Spirit is. Drunkenness is common in our day. Everyone knows something about this illustration. I believe Paul brings drunkenness in as an illustration to make some things about

146

the fullness of the Spirit clear. Here is a man and here is a drink. The man knows that there is something in that drink which has a design for control. He is not ignorant as to its eventual effect if he drinks enough of it. He willfully takes into his body the drink. It enters his bloodstream quickly. If he drinks enough of it there is a strange thing which takes place in the body metabolism. The alcohol is carried in the bloodstream to the brain areas and the man's whole thinking is affected. He is alcohol-filled, controlled, saturated, intoxicated. He can stay that way by continuing to drink. And if he is drunk long enough and continues to experience alcoholic intake, he will begin to see things, hear things, and experience things that nobody else sees, hears, or experiences. He is drunk. "Don't be drunk," Paul implores, "But be filled with the Spirit."

"Be filled with the Spirit" is the positive command. The negative has paved the way for it. Is it wrong to be drunk with wine? It is, because there is a positive command against it! Then it is wrong not to be filled with the Spirit. There is a positive command for it. Which is the most wrong? Before God the wrongness is not guaged as we would measure it. The social consequences may vary, but the wrongness of sin is not measured in degrees of seriousness. It is wrong to be drunk with wine and it is just as wrong not to be filled with the Spirit. Would you tolerate a pastor who came to the pulpit in a drunken condition to deliver the Sunday morning sermon? You should be just as concerned about one who comes to deliver his message not filled with the Spirit. Mother, would you cherish the thought of an intoxicated Sunday School teacher standing before your child on Sunday morning in Sunday School? Then you should be just as concerned that the teacher who teaches your children be filled with the Spirit of God.

Word Study

The word for "filled" is defined in *Thayer's Greek Lexicon* thusly: "That which wholly takes possession of the mind is said to fill it." It is further defined "to accomplish, to fill full, to carry out to the full, to control."

Pentecost, in his splendid book, *Pattern for maturity,* states in his chapter on the fullness of the Spirit, "The common concept which is basic to all of these words is the thought of filling up a vessel by putting something into it. An empty glass into which water is poured is said to be filled with water. Now, of course, it would be a mistake to say that the glass is empty. For unless it is in a vacuum, it is not empty at all; it is filled with air. And the water that is poured into that glass drives out what previously had been filling and fills it with something new. And when the apostle speaks of being filled with the Spirit, he is speaking of the Spirit supplanting that which was once within, then taking over so that the person is filled with the Spirit of God."

Let us look at several usages of the word for fullness in the New Testament. In Luke 5:26 we read that they were filled with fear. In Acts 6:5 Stephen is described as a man full of faith and of the Holy Spirit. In Acts 2:4 the folks in the upper room were all filled with the Holy Spirit. In Acts 5:3 Peter asks Annanias, "Why hath Satan filled your heart to lie to the Holy Ghost?" So we see that the word carries with it the implication of influence, control, and guidance. A man may be controlled by the adversary or controlled by the Lord. He can be influenced by alcohol or be filled with the Holy Spirit. What he is filled with is what controls him.

Grammatical Implications

The Greek is a wonderful and exacting language. Its tenses are clear and the implications are significant. The command, "Be filled" is one word in the Greek language and carries some vital implications within the construction of that word. Let us look at them.

First, it is *plural* in number. All of the Ephesians were involved in this command. It was not for an elite few, but for all. The fullness of the Spirit is for everyone.

Second, it is *present* in tense. Thus, it should be read . . . "Be always being filled with the Spirit." The present tense is best described by a continuing line. The emphasis is laid on continuing. We will see just how significant this is later on in this chapter.

Third, it is *passive* in voice. This means that the subject does not do the acting, but it receives the action. Being filled with the Spirit is not something we do. It is something that we allow God to do. We are not to be passive in our attitude toward experiencing the fullness, but we are to understand that it is something we allow God to accomplish in us as we meet the requirements.

Fourth, it is *imperative* in mood. It is a command. Being filled with the Spirit is not an option that the God-pleasing Christian has. He is either filled with the Spirit or he lives short of the plan of God for his life.

Being *plural* in number, *present* in tense, *passive* in voice and *imperative* in mood, this command could properly be read: "All of you, be always being filled with the Spirit all the time."

For our study here we will look at the fullness of the Spirit under four descriptive lights. One, it is *a truth to be believed;* two, *a revelation to be received;* three, *an experience to be had;* and four, *a relationship to be continued.*

A Truth to Be Believed

The fullness of the Spirit is a plain, primary, pivotal truth in the New Testament. It would be a truth if Ephesians 5:18 were the only reference to it. There are many others.

The angel told of the birth of John the Baptist, "He shall be filled with the Holy Ghost from his mother's womb" (Luke 1:15). I would not have minded being his baby-sitter!

In the same chapter, verse 41, his mother, Elizabeth was filled with the Holy Ghost when she heard the salutation of Mary, her cousin.

In the same chapter, verse 67, Zacharias, the father of John the Baptist, was filled with the Holy Ghost.

In Luke 4:1 Jesus is described as having been "full of the Holy Ghost" after his baptism. Being full of the Spirit, He was led of the Spirit into the wilderness.

In Acts 2:4 the disciples were all filled with the Spirit.

In Acts 4:8 Peter made answer to the query of his opposition while he was "filled with the Holy Ghost."

In Acts 4:31 they were praying in a certain place and it was shaken by the power of God. They were all filled with the Holy Ghost.

In Acts 9:17 Paul was filled with the Spirit after his conversion experience under the ministry of Ananias.

The deacons elected in Acts 6 were to be men full of the Holy Spirit. They were to be qualified by the control of God in their lives.

In Acts 13:9 Paul, as he faced the sorcerer, was "filled with the Holy Ghost."

In our text we are implored to be filled with the Spirit.

Earlier in the book of Ephesians we read these words: "That ye might be filled with all the fulness of God" (Eph. 3:19).

It is a truth with which we must reckon. It is not likely that God will reveal anything to your heart if you are not willing to accept it as a truth. This is a truth for your family. It is vital to the building up of your home as one home under God.

A Revelation to Be Received

I have just recently begun to fully realize that a man cannot experience a truth. He can believe it, but he cannot experience it. *Truth* is to be believed. A *revelation* may be experienced. You can read a truth on a printed page or hear a truth from someone's lips. But hearing it or even seeing it with your eyes is not enough. The Spirit-filled life is a truth indeed. But to experience it, there must be a revelation. A *truth* can be shared from mind to mind. A *revelation* is shared from Spirit to spirit. Many across the nation are seeing the wisdom of being filled with the Spirit. They are eagerly asking how it might be received. Sometimes they are introduced to a plan, a method, or a procedure. They are told that if they say this, do that, or react in this fashion, they will be filled. I am for instruction in every sense of the word, but it should be remembered that being filled with the Spirit is not a matter of just going through a set of steps. *It is a revelation of God from his Spirit to your spirit.* Now, I am convinced that when we are open and ready, God will make that revelation known to us. Being saved is likewise a revelation to be received. It takes an act of God to get somebody saved and it takes an act of God to get somebody filled with the Spirit.

It is a revelation expressed in the scripture and confirmed in the spirit of man. Just to realize that one needs to be filled is not enough. Just to desire to be filled is not enough. When the revelation is appropriated then there will be fullness. You may be saying, "I don't know what you are talking about!" That is fine. Just hold these words in your heart. There will be a time when you will know. You may not even know how to say what you know, or why you know, or how you know, but you will know that you know. It will then be a revelation, the work of the Holy Spirit.

An Experience to Be Had

Though the command to be filled in Ephesians 5:18 is in the continuous present tense, it is understood that in order to continue to be filled one must have been filled in the first place. There are as many kinds of experiences as there are different dispositions. It is a mistake to predict the emotional feelings that may accompany the filling experience just as it is a mistake to do the same with the salvation experience. Emotions are fine in their place, but their place is not to gauge the validity of an experience. There may, in fact, be no emotions accompanying a spiritual experience.

The three blind men were all healed and went away seeing. Vance Havner suggests that if they lived today, there would be an immediate problem. The first blind man would say, "Jesus just touched me and I saw straightway." The second might reply, "My friend, I am sorry, but your experience is not genuine or orthodox. You see, He touched me once and I could see, but not very well, and He touched me again and I saw clearly." To which the third man would reply, "Men, you're both wrong. Your experiences could not be genuine. He made a mixture of clay and spittle and sent me to wash in the Pool of Siloam and then I could see." Dr. Havner suggests that if those blind men lived today, there would be three denominations before the week was out . . . the *one-touch church,* the *two-touch church,* and the *mud-in-the-eye church.* Our experiences will not be the same.

Being filled with the Spirit is an experience. It is a mistake to predict or demand the emotions or reactions that will accompany the experience. For some it may be quite matter-of-fact. For others it may be quite traumatic. For still others it may be with deep feeling, but not much outward emotion.

It is generally an experience which is accompanied by some desperation. Sickened by failure and a sense of sin, many a person has come to admit that he cannot go on without a work of grace in his heart. The Holy Spirit has responded and met them at the point of their need, and glorious has been the result.

It is an initial experience, a continuing experience, and a repeated experience. To be a present tense it must have been initiated at a given point of time. It is a vital question to ask if one has been filled with the Spirit. It is just as vital to ask if one is being filled with the Spirit now.

The fullness of the Spirit in its beginning is that sovereign work of the Spirit of God by which, on the occasion of our faith, He takes control of our whole beings and begins to make us living demonstrations of the will of God. It seems to be common today to confuse the baptism of the Spirit with the fullness of the Spirit. Without giving space for a lengthy discussion allow some brief observations. The *baptism* of the Spirit is the initial work of the Spirit of God by which, on the occasion of our repentance and faith, we are placed into Jesus Christ and He into us. The *fullness* of the Spirit is the continuing and controlling work of the Spirit within us. The *baptism* of the Spirit secures *relationship* with God. The *fullness* of the Spirit secures *fellowship*. The *baptism* of the Spirit gives us *position* in Christ. The *fullness* of the Spirit gives us *power* through Christ. The *baptism* of the Spirit brings us to victory over the *penalty of sin*. The *fullness* of the Spirit brings us to victory over the *power of sin*.

The fullness of the Spirit is an experience. Ideally, the new convert should be immediately taught about the meaning of the fullness of the Spirit. At salvation the Spirit of God enters the heart of the convert. He is immediately indwelt with the Holy Spirit. At least for a brief time he is, in a real sense, under the control of the Spirit. If he is properly instructed as to what happened inside him at conversion, he will walk on into the glory of the life of fullness. For most of us this was not the experience. There was backsliding, defeat, disillusionment, and desperation. God was bringing us to a fresh revelation of the meaning of our salvation. It is not so much that we received something in the fullness as it is that we came to realize what we have had all along in the glory of an indwelling Lord.

A Relationship to Be Continued

The significance of the present tense in Ephesians 5:18 is to be discovered in this fact of a continuing relationship. An experience is virtually worthless unless it leads to a meaningful and fulfilling relationship. The experience is the gateway; the relationship is the glory. If we glory in an experience, we will miss the issue of the whole matter. The work of the Holy Spirit is to reveal the Lord Jesus Christ in us. We have not arrived when we are filled with the Spirit. We have just really commenced.

It is a relationship of *obedience*. The Holy Spirit will exact from you total obedience. He will not tolerate in you the slightest deviation. Things will be brought to mind that you never attached much seriousness to before. Now the Holy Spirit is obliged to bring the smallest disobedience to your attention. When obedience ceases, fullness ceases. Disobedience is sin. Sin breaks fellowship. Broken fellowship means that the flow of fulness is lost. It may be restored when sin is confessed and made right.

It is a relationship of *discipline*. The exercise of discipline serves to keep our attention on spiritual things and to keep us in condition for usefulness. The root word for discipline is disciple. The disciple is a learner. We learn through the exercise of control over our minds and bodies. God reveals Himself to His disciples.

It is a relationship of *purging*. Jesus said in John 15 that God would purge the branch that was bearing fruit, that it might bring forth more fruit. Many people, upon entering the life of the Spirit, begin to experience some divine purging and, not having been instructed of its meaning, bolt and run. God is ever bringing us through processes in order to render us more fruitful. Purging is the doing away with what we can do without in order to bear more fruit.

It is a relationship of *growth*. Many have a vital experience with the Holy Spirit and enter into such joyous emotion, such lifting of spirit, such victory of life that they suppose that they have reached that place of total and permanent victory. They are convinced that they are now full grown. Being filled with the Spirit does not stop spiritual growth or complete it. It simply puts it on a proper schedule.

As we walk in the Spirit, there is growth.

The stages through which we pass on the way to the fullness are generally as follows:

I ought to be . . . . . . the demand.
I want to be . . . . . . the desired.
I must be . . . . . . the desperation.
I will be . . . . . . the decision.

It is not enough to just feel a sense of oughtness. Nor is it sufficient to have a desire. The desperation can be real, but unless there comes a positive decision, the fulness cannot come.

"Fill me, Holy Spirit, fill me,
All thy filling would I know.
I am smallest of thy vessels,
Yet, I much can overflow."

LEWIS SPERRY CHAFER

Will you pass through those gates right now? As you have believed the truth, opened yourself for the revelation, desired the experience, and have been willing to be involved in an eternal relationship, will you now allow him to do it . . . to fill you with His blessed Holy Spirit. Will you now confess your sins? Will you now make a choice against your old self? Will you now reckon yourself dead indeed unto sin, but alive unto God through Christ? Will you choose the will of God for your life, crowning Jesus Christ as your sovereign Lord? You will welcome another dimension into your life . . . the dimension of divine control, the fulness of the Spirit.

Fullness for the Family

When individuals begin to discover the fullness of the Spirit, they find that no area of life remains untouched. The family life will come under intense investigation by the Holy Spirit. Hidden feelings, roots of bitterness, and little feelings will no longer be tolerated. The Spirit will bring these to the surface where they can be faced and dealt with.

Only through the power of the Holy Spirit can the family be brought into such a position as to be one home under God. Just as he brings the individual to fullness, he can reign in the atmosphere of the home so completely that the home is indivisible. There will be struggles and battles, but with these there will be successes and victories.

The Spirit-filled life is not a life without warfare. It is simply the life of Jesus Christ, our Lord, made real by his Spirit in the arena of life. The family is the proving ground for demonstration of the fullness of the Spirit.

There is a sense in which this chapter should have been the first chapter of this volume. But for one consideration, it would have been chapter 1. A few more pages and you will lay this volume aside. What you have read last will influence your future hours and days more than what you read first. You have read these pages with a mixture of responses including interest, puzzlement, wonder, anger, frustration, conviction, and desire. I trust that the last response you have as you finish this volume is that of desire. Add to that desire a good measure of determination and right here make this affirmation:

If there is only one home left on earth that is under God, I declare that I want it to be my home. I am willing to pay whatever price is necessary, make any adjustments called for, and take whatever steps divinely commanded to have a home that is Spirit-filled. Take over me and take over my home. In Jesus' name, Amen!

> Father, by this blessed filling,
> Dwell Thyself in us we pray!
> We are waiting, Thou art willing!
> Fill us with Thyself today!

Our prayer for you, dear reader, is that God may make the truths on these pages live in your family as they have come alive in ours. With this book go the prayers of the Taylors for all who pick it up to read.

JACK, BARBARA, TAMMY, AND TIMMY TAYLOR

Perspective: To Be Continued . . .

I have never particularly cherished the words "The End." When I see them, I think of the regrets of all the times when something I didn't want to cease came to . . . the end. I think that the most wonderful thing about this business of being a Christian and a part of the family of God is just this: We don't ever have to face the end! Yes, there will be the end of relationships as we know them. There will be the end of all that can be brought to an end. But there are some things that are eternal.

We will one day discover to our delight that God's plan for the family was to *fit us for the future,* to *equip us for eternity.* Being a part of our earthly family and bringing that family to a right position under the authority of God was just a test run for heaven.

Therefore, the subject of this volume cannot come to an end. It is . . . *to be continued.* Earthly relationships will give way to heavenly ones, and there will always be the family of God. A hundred billion years from today, if time were measured, the caption could still be the same . . . *to be continued.*

It is from this perspective that I challenge you today, right now, to begin what can never be ended . . . "one home under God."

Other Broadman Books
by
Jack R. Taylor

The Key to Triumphant Living
Much More!
Victory Over the Devil